Reiki for a New Millennium

Notice to Prospective Students

The ability to channel Reiki energy cannot be learned by reading a book. This ability is transferred to the student by the Reiki Master during an attunement process. Reiki attunements are given as a standard part of Reiki training. It is suggested that if you would like to learn Reiki, you should contact a competent Reiki teacher. A list of Reiki teachers can be provided by contacting the International Center for Reiki Training through Vision Publications.

ISBN 1-886785-02-3

Library of Congress Catalog Card Number: 98-87939

Vision Publications
21421 Hilltop St., #28, Southfield, MI 48034 USA
Phone (800) 332-8112, (248) 948-8112 Fax (248) 948-9534
E-mail center@reiki.org web site www.reiki.org

Contents

Introduction i
Reiki, Ancient Miracle for Modern Times 1
Dr. Usui's Gift 8
Reiki, Questions and Answers 13
The Usui Reiki Symbols 22
Are Your Usui Reiki Symbols Accurate? 28
Strengthen Your Reiki Energy 29
Developing Your Reiki Practice 36
The Promise of a Developing Reiki Practice 37
Becoming a Reiki Master 48
Issues of Time and Money 55
Reiki and Legal Issues 60
Reiki for Success 63
Reiki Research 67
Reiki in Hospitals 76
Was Jesus a Reiki Master? 87
Reiki as a Spiritual Path 92
Reiki for Peace 99
World Peace Crystal Grid Placed at the North Pole 103
The Changing Way of Reiki 110
The Original Reiki Ideals 115
Discovering the Roots of Reiki 119
Reiki, A New Direction 129
The Greatest Healing the World has Ever Known 138
The International Center for Reiki Training 148
The Center Philosophy 152
The Center Purpose 153
Additional Books and Literature on Healing 155
Index 163

Introduction

We are experiencing the changing of the ages and this has more meaning than just a number on the calendar. Great change is taking place in the world. We are in the middle of a global transformation that is affecting every aspect of life. This process is creating fear and uncertainty for some, but for others, it presents a wonderful opportunity. The world as we have known it is dying and a new one is emerging. Those who are able to let go of old ways will enjoy the process and be able to contribute to the greatest experience the world has ever known -- the birth of a new age. As part of this process, ancient knowledge is becoming available to assist us. Reiki is a technique that can foster the qualities in us necessary to easily make the transition and create the unity and love that will be the essence of the new millennium.

Aspects of Change

Scientific discoveries and new technologies constantly coming into use along with the increase in world population are creating a situation unlike any this planet has seen before. The very premise on which civilization is based is about to shift, altering the fabric of society itself. The awesome number and rate of change taking place, even when positive, is becoming increasingly difficult to deal with. This is true on a global scale, and in our personal lives. Stress in society is at an all time high.

The world population has increased to over six billion people, with the last billion added in just eleven years! The acceleration in growth of the human population is having a positive affect on the global economy by greatly increasing the need for food, shelter and other commodities, while at the same time, depleting our vital resources and creating pollution problems.

The speed and power of computers is doubling every 18 months. Computers currently in use by millions of people all over the world are more powerful than those available only to Universities and large research groups a few years ago. Communication technology is also improving at a phenomenal rate. Satellite TV, facsimile machines, cell phones and email are evolving rapidly. Over 100 million Internet users are now making instant, low cost communications all over the world — and the number of users continues to grow! It is projected that by the year 2002 there will be over 350 million users worldwide. The speed of the Internet is about to increase by 50 to 100 times its present rate, making real time video, music and other enhanced forms of entertainment a reality. All over the planet, Personal TV stations, virtual reality as well as a multitude of unthought of technologies are about to become available. All of this is stimulating a greater sense of interconnectedness between people and is causing us to change the way we look at the world. We are starting to accept the world in its wholeness, rather than thinking of it as composed of separate and often opposing parts.

As the Piscean Age yields to Aquarius, we are also going through changes on a metaphysical level. The consciousness of the Piscean age is characterized by the dependence of the masses on an authority figure to whom they surrender their power. Monarchies, dictatorships and religious and corporate hierarchies reflect this Piscean paradigm. In the area of spiritual practices, we see this in the structure of the Catholic church as well as most other western and many Eastern religions. A "one size fits all" mentality is imposed from the top with one formula of conduct prescribed for the followers below. As we move into the Aquarian Age, individuals will connect directly with God and receive guidance specific to their unique needs. At the same time they will be guided to interact harmoniously with all others. Greater freedom in spiritual and religious expression will abound.

Rather than one religion needing to dominate all others to bring world peace, peace will come because all religions and spiritual paths will honor and respect each other and work together for peace. However, society will undergo a profound transformation in its values, beliefs and motivations as well as the way it is organized as we move from where we currently are to a firmly established new world of peace.

On a more personal level, corporate downsizing, mergers and buyouts are causing employees to change jobs more frequently and often relocate to a new part of the country. One, two or more career changes in a lifetime are now often necessary. Marriages are also ending more quickly, burdening the marriage partners and their children with greater hardships and difficulties.

The AIDS epidemic, Ebola, the resurgence of TB and the appearance of new diseases are creating more complex health problems. While modern medical technology is often helpful, it can be very expensive and is often the source of new problems.

The number of challenges and crisis situations in the world is likely to increase before integration on a new level of harmony is complete. While many of these changes are considered to be unwanted problems, they will ultimately be seen as necessary and beneficial. Many will consider them to be part of a planetary healing crisis and an integral part of the stress that accompanies positive change.

Reiki Reduces the Stress of Change

As technology continues to develop and increase in use, people are experiencing major imbalances in their personal lives. Human needs are going unfulfilled and a backlash is developing. To create balance, they are seeking ways to express and nurture their human side. Interest in spiritual things, including the practice of Reiki, is increasing.

Reiki is a Japanese technique for stress reduction and relaxation that also promotes healing. It uses no technology at all and is an effective method of gaining balance in our modern lives. It can help alleviate many of the problems our transforming society is creating and also stimulate feelings of love, peace, harmony, joy and all the other qualities needed in the new millennium.

Based on subtle life energy that flows through ones hands, a Reiki treatment produces a warm glowing radiance that nurtures and restores vitality. It is a wonderful feeling. Reiki treatments consistently demonstrate their positive affects to promote health and happiness as well as improve every aspect of human activity.

In its long history of use, Reiki has been known to help or heal every malady known to humanity. In addition, it is used by healthy people to increase happiness, enhance productivity and stimulate creative energy. Reiki can be self-administered as well as used to treat others. One of the most amazing things about Reiki is that it can be sent at a distance to help others or directed to global crises.

With over one million practitioners in the US and even more around the world, Reiki is fast becoming a universal solution for the many challenges we face.

Reiki is a powerful, yet compassionate technique for these challenging times! It enables us to participate directly in the transformation of the world. I invite you to make use of this amazing opportunity!

In the following pages, you will discover the enormous potential of Reiki to solve personal problems and usher in the new millennium. A wide range of topics are addressed and the many facets of Reiki are explained. Much of this material first appeared as articles in the *Reiki News*.

The Japanese kanji for Reiki

Reiki, Ancient Miracle for Modern Times

The knowledge that an unseen energy flows through all living things and directly affects the quality of health has been part of the wisdom of many cultures since ancient times. The existence of this "life energy" has been verified by recent scientific experiments and medical doctors are considering the role it plays in the functioning of the immune system and the healing process. Because of this, it is becoming a more widely accepted concept.

Reiki, a technique for stress reduction that also promotes healing, allows everyone to tap into an unlimited supply of "life energy." Thought to have originated in Tibet thousands of years ago, Reiki was rediscovered by Dr. Mikao Usui, a Japanese Buddhist early in the 20th Century.

Reiki is administered by laying-on hands. A standard treatment includes hand positions around the head, shoulders, stomach, legs and feet. The client does not disrobe and usually lays on a massage or Reiki table. The hands can be placed in contact with the person or the treatment can be given with the hands a few inches away from the body. A treatment usually takes between 45 minutes to an hour and a half and feels like a wonderful glowing radiance that flows through you and surrounds you. Treatments can be given to others as well as to oneself. Reiki treats the whole person including body, emotions, mind and spirit and creates many beneficial affects including relaxation and feelings of peace, security and well-being. Many have reported miraculous healing's.

Reiki is a simple, natural and safe method of spiritual healing and self-improvement that everyone can use. It has been effective in

Dr. Mikao Usui ("Usui Sensei"),
founder of the Usui Reiki System of Healing

helping virtually every known illness and malady and always creates a beneficial effect. However, Reiki is not a substitute for regular medical or psychological care, but works in conjunction with them to relieve side effects and promote healing. In fact, some hospitals and doctor's offices are beginning to integrate it into patient care. (see the chapter on Reiki in Hospitals on page 76)

An amazingly simple technique to learn, the ability to use Reiki is not taught in the usual sense, but is transferred to the student when attending a Reiki class. This ability is passed on during an "attunement" given by a Reiki Master and allows the student to tap into an unlimited supply of "life force energy" to improve one's health and enhance the quality of life.

There is very little to memorize or learn in order to do Reiki. Once one has taken a Reiki class and received an attunement, all that is necessary is to place ones hands on another or on oneself and Reiki healing energy automatically begins to flow. One does not have to have a background in spiritual or metaphysical training as no previous experience is necessary. Because of this, the ability to do Reiki is available to everyone. It has been successfully taught to people of all ages and backgrounds. There are now well over one million people who practice Reiki world wide and the numbers keep growing.

The word Reiki is composed of two Japanese words - Rei and Ki. When translating Japanese into English we must keep in mind that an exact translation is difficult. The Japanese language has many levels of meaning. Therefore the context in which the word is being used must be kept in mind when attempting to communicate its essence. Because these words are used in a spiritual healing context, a Japanese/English dictionary does not provide the depth of meaning we seek, as its definitions are based on common, everyday Japanese. As an example , Rei is often defined as ghost and Ki as vapor and while these words vaguely point in the direction of meaning we seek, they fall far short of the understanding that is needed.

When seeking a definition from a more spiritual context, we find that Rei can be defined as the Higher Intelligence that guides the creation and functioning of the universe. Rei is a subtle wisdom that permeates everything, both animate and inanimate. This subtle wisdom guides the evolution of all creation ranging from the unfolding of galaxies to the development of life. On a human level, it is available to help us in times of need and to act as a source of guidance in our lives. Because of its infinite nature, it is all knowing. Rei is also called God and has many other names depending on the culture that has identified it.

Ki is the nonphysical energy that animates all living things. Ki is flowing in everything that is alive including plants, animals and humans. When a person's Ki is high, they will feel strong, confident, and ready to enjoy life and take on its challenges. When it is low, they will feel weak and are more likely to get sick. We receive Ki from the air we breathe, from food, sunshine, and from sleep. It is also possible to increase our Ki by using breathing exercises and meditation. When a person dies, their Ki leaves the physical body. Ki is also the Chi of China, the prana of India, the Ti or Ki of Hawaii, and has also been called odic force, orgone, bioplasma and life force.

With the above information in mind, Reiki can be defined as a nonphysical healing energy made up of life force energy that is guided by the Higher Intelligence, or spiritually guided life force energy. This is a functional definition as it closely parallels the experiences of those who practice Reiki in that Reiki energy seems to have an intelligence of its own, flowing where it is needed in the client and creating the healing conditions necessary for the individuals needs. It cannot be guided by the mind, therefore, it is not limited by the experience or ability of the practitioner. Neither can it be misused as it always creates a healing effect. (It must be kept in mind that Reiki is not the same as simple life force energy as life force energy by itself can be influenced by the mind and because of this, can create benefits as well as cause problems including ill health if improperly guided. This is why Reiki is safe - it is always guided by the Higher Power.)

How Reiki Heals

The primary source or cause of health comes from the Ki that flows through and around the individual rather than from the functional condition of the physical organs and tissues. It is Ki that animates the physical organs and tissues as it flows through them and therefore is responsible for creating a healthy condition. If the flow of Ki is disrupted, the physical organs and tissues will be adversely affected. Therefore, it is a disruption in the flow of Ki that is the main cause of illness.

An important attribute of Ki is that it responds to ones thoughts and feelings. Ki will flow more strongly or be weakened in its action depending on the quality of ones thoughts and feelings. It is our negative thoughts and feelings that are the main cause of restriction in the flow of Ki. All negative or disharmonious thoughts or feelings will cause a disruption in the flow of Ki. Even western medicine recognizes the role played by the mind in creating illness and some western doctors state that as much as 98% of illness is caused directly or indirectly by the mind.

It must be understood that the mind exists not only in the brain, but also throughout the body. The nervous system extends to every organ and tissue in the body and so the mind exists there also. It is also known that the mind extends outside the body in a subtle energy field two to three feet thick called the aura. Because of this, it is more appropriate to call our mind a mind/body as the mind and body are so closely linked.

Therefore, our thoughts including those that cause ill health are not just in the brain, but also collect in various locations throughout the body and in the aura. The places where negative thoughts and feelings collect is where Ki is restricted in its flow and this causes the physical organs that exist at these locations to be restricted in their functioning as well. If these negative thoughts and feelings are not eliminated, over time illness could develop.

The thoughts and feelings in our conscious minds are important, but those in our unconscious mind are even more important. They create the greatest problem as they are more able to directly influence the flow of Ki. Fortunately, Reiki works on the unconscious levels of our mind/body as well and will heal these negative thoughts thus restoring the natural flow of Ki.

The great value of Reiki is that because it is guided by the Higher Intelligence, it knows exactly where to go and how to respond to restrictions in the flow of Ki. It can work directly in the unconscious parts of the mind/body which contain negative Ki-inhibiting thoughts and feelings and eliminate them. As Reiki flows through a sick or unhealthy area, it breaks up and washes away any negative thoughts or feelings lodged in the unconscious mind/body thus allowing a normal healthy flow of Ki to resume. As this happens, the unhealthy physical organs and tissues become properly nourished with Ki and begin functioning in a balanced healthy way thus replacing illness with health.

This non-invasive, completely benign healing technique is becoming more and more popular. As western medicine continues to explore alternative methods of healing, Reiki is beginning to play an important role as an accepted and valued healing practice.

Dr. Usui's Gift

Reiki is truly one of the most wonderful things present on the planet at this time. Its positive attributes are many and it is important to clearly understand them in order to fully appreciate just how valuable Reiki is. If we ignore or do not clearly understand its potential, then we may not take the necessary action to fully experience its value.

This is important for us now as we enter a new millennium as conditions on the planet are critical. There are wars, famines, disease, over population, pollution, the destruction of the ecosystem, crime, poverty and horrible living conditions for many. These problems are being experienced by billions of people and are getting worse. These problems have been caused primarily by the decisions people have made on an individual, local and global basis.

The underlying values and beliefs which govern the decision making processes for the planet are in need of a major revision. We need to change our values and beliefs so we can move from a fragmented earth to a whole earth, from an earth motivated by fear to an earth motivated by love, from an earth filled with suspicion and conflict to an earth living in trust and cooperation,

Within Reiki lies the energy and ability necessary to make these changes. As the number of Reiki practitioners grows, Reiki is becoming a potential factor in solving the problems of the world, and facilitating the shift to world peace and harmony that is needed, but only if Reiki is used wisely.

Lets look at some of the qualities that Reiki possesses so we can more clearly understand the role it can play in global healing. Reiki is a spiritual healing technique that is unique. When we look at other healing techniques, we find that often years of practice are necessary in order to develop skill. Many of these other techniques are like martial arts requiring discipline, focus, meditative skill and natural ability in order to do well.

However, unlike other healing techniques, Reiki does not require discipline or years of training to receive healing ability. Rather, Reiki comes to us as a gift. (This is true for the practitioner levels as well as for the Master or teaching level wherein one can pass Reiki on to others.) The ability to do Reiki comes immediately to the student upon receiving the attunement. During the attunement, the ability to channel Reiki comes from the Higher Power, passes through the Reiki teacher and into the student. The attunement energy is guided by the Higher Power and makes adjustments within itself for each student so that each receives exactly what they need in order to begin channeling Reiki. During the attunement, the Higher Power actually adjusts and heals the students chakras and energy field and connects the student directly to the source of Reiki. After the attunement, all that is necessary for the student to channel healing energy is to place one's hands on oneself or a client and the healing energy begins flowing automatically. This gift is a direct expression of grace from the Higher Power. Because of this, the attunement process is a very sacred and spiritual experience.

When one does Reiki healing, the energy is guided by the Higher Power and does not require direction from the practitioner.

Therefore, there is no concern about whether the healing is being done properly as the Higher Power always guides the healing energy in a way that is exactly appropriate for the client. Because the Higher Power is guiding the healing process, the practitioner cannot take responsibility for the results. Therefore, one's ego is not so easily inflated by the healing and it is much easier for both the practitioner and client to give full credit to the Higher Power for the value that is received. This process encourages one to trust in the Higher Power, thus enhancing one's spiritual growth.

Because the ability to receive Reiki is free of any requirements on the part of the student, all that is necessary is for the student to want to receive the ability and for the student to attend a Reiki class and receive the attunement. Because of this, the ability to do Reiki can be received quickly by anyone during a weekend class.

Another wonderful aspect of Reiki healing is that the energy does not come from the practitioner, but comes from the unlimited source, the Higher Power. This means that the practitioner's energy is never depleted. In fact, a practitioner's energy level actually increases when she or he channels Reiki. This is because the Higher Power considers both the practitioner and the client to be in need of healing and both receive a treatment. Therefore, the practitioner always feels better after giving a Reiki treatment!

In Reiki II a person receives the ability to send Reiki treatments to others at a distance. This allows them to treat others no matter where they are located. It is also possible to send Reiki to heal negative situations and for whole groups of people to work together to send at the same time, thus greatly increasing the effectiveness. Using this technique, it is possible for large numbers of

Reiki practitioners to pool their channeled energy and send Reiki to local and world trouble spots thus creating a significant contribution toward solving global problems.

It is clear from the above description that Reiki is a healing force of unprecedented value. It can be learned quickly by anyone, is guided by the Higher Power, does not deplete the practitioner's energy, can be used to treat self and others and can be sent at a distance to heal others or sent by groups to heal local and global situations. The essence of Reiki healing energy is love, peace, harmony, cooperation and trust, therefore, it contains the very qualities that are needed to solve the problems of the earth. The fact that Reiki can be learned quickly by anyone makes it a natural solution for the suffering now being experienced all around us. If Reiki is learned by enough people and those people work together to send Reiki to local and global problems those problems can be turned around and this will promote a condition of harmony and peace among the world's people. In this way, Reiki will be acting to achieve the most important goal of the new millennium.

It is the purpose of The International Center for Reiki Training to act on this awareness and focus its resources to make Reiki available to all people who want it and to inspire and motivate them to actively use Reiki to solve personal, local and global challenges. In order to do this we actively promote the following conditions.

1. Cooperation between all Reiki practitioners and organizations. Before Reiki can bring harmony to the earth, there must be harmony between all Reiki healers.

2. Reasonable fees for all levels so that everyone can learn it.

3. Well organized classes.

4. Motivation for all Reiki practitioners to work together to use Reiki regularly to solve personal, local and global challenges.

In order to promote the above conditions, The Center has opened a web site on the Internet at www.reiki.org. Anyone with a computer and software can connect to the Web and make use of our web site. Our web site will be making Reiki information available to everyone and be facilitating the focus of distant Reiki to solve global challenges.

Your Responsibility to Heal

While Reiki energy comes to us as a gift, in order to gain its full benefit, one must take responsibility for one's healing and self-improvement. This means that one must be willing, with the help of Reiki, to learn the lessons that one's problems and/or illnesses have to offer, have the willingness to grow and be dedicated to one's life purpose. A change in one's habits, attitudes and often one's beliefs are necessary if lasting benefits are to come.

Reiki, Questions and Answers

Q. Where does Reiki energy come from?
A. Reiki energy is a subtle energy. It is different than electricity or chemical energy or other kinds of physical energy. Reiki energy comes from the Higher Power, which exists on a higher dimension than the physical world we are familiar with. When viewed clairvoyantly, Reiki energy appears to come down from above and to enter the top of the practitioners head after which if flows through the body and out the hands. It appears to flow this way because of our perspective. However, the true source of Reiki energy is within ourselves. .

Q. Is Reiki a Religion?
A. Although Reiki energy is spiritual in nature, Reiki is not a religion. Practitioners are not asked to change any religious or spiritual beliefs they may have. They are free to continue believing anything they choose and are encouraged to make their own decisions concerning the nature of their religious practices.

Q. How is a Reiki treatment given?
A. In a standard treatment Reiki energy flows from the practitioners hands into the client. The client is usually laying on a massage table but treatments can also be given while the client is seated or even standing. The client remains fully clothed. The practitioner places her/his hands on or near the clients body in a series of hand positions. These include positions around the head and shoulders, the stomach, and feet. Other, more specific positions may be used based on the clients needs. Each position is held for three to ten minutes depending on how much Reiki the client

needs at each position. The whole treatment usually lasts between 45 and 90 minutes.

Q. What does a Reiki treatment feel like?
A. What one experiences during a Reiki treatment varies somewhat from person to person. However, feelings of deep relaxation are usually felt by all. In addition, many feel a wonderful glowing radiance that flows through and surrounds the them. As the Reiki energy encourages one to let go of all tension, anxiety, fear or other negative feelings a state of peace and well-being is experienced. Some drift off to sleep or report floating outside their bodies or have visions and other mystical experiences. At the end of the treatment, one feels refreshed with a more positive, balanced outlook.

Q. What can be treated with Reiki?
A. Reiki has had a positive affect on all forms of illness and negative conditions. This includes minor things like head or stomach aches, bee stings, colds, flu, tension and anxiety as well as serious illness like heart disease, cancer, leukemia, etc. The side effects of regular medical treatments have also been reduced or eliminated. This includes the negative effects of chemotherapy, post operative pain and depression as well as improving the healing rate and reducing the time needed to stay in the hospital. Reiki always helps and in some cases people have experienced complete healings which have been confirmed by medical tests before and after the Reiki treatments. However, while some have experienced miracles, they cannot be guaranteed. Stress reduction with some improvement in ones physical and psychological condition are what most experience.

Q. Does one have to stop seeing a regular doctor or psychologist in order to receive a Reiki treatment?
A. No. Reiki works in conjunction with regular medical or psychological treatment. If one has a medical or psychological condition, it is recommended that one see a licensed health care professional in addition to receiving Reiki treatments. Reiki energy works in harmony with all other forms of healing, including drugs, surgery, psychological care or any other method of alternative care and will improve the results.

Q. Who can learn to do Reiki?
A. Reiki is a very simple technique to learn and is not dependent on one having any prior experience with healing, meditation or any other kind of training. It has be successfully learned by over one million people from all walks of life, both young an old. The reason it is so easy to learn that it is not taught in the usual way something is taught. The ability to do Reiki is simply transferred from the teacher to the student through a process called an attunement that takes place during a Reiki class. As soon as one receives an attunement, they have the ability to do Reiki and after that whenever one places their hands on themselves or on another person with the intention of doing Reiki, the healing energy will automatically begin flowing.

Q. How long does it take to learn Reiki?
A. A beginning Reiki class is taught on a weekend. The class can be one or two days long. I recommend that the minimum time necessary be at least six to seven hours. Along with the attunement, it is necessary that the student be shown how to give treatments and also to practice giving treatments in class.

Q. What is a Reiki attunement?

A. A Reiki attunement is the process by which a person receives the ability to give Reiki treatments. The attunement is administered by the Reiki Master during the Reiki class. During the attunement, the Reiki Master will touch the students head, shoulders, and hands and use one or more special breathing techniques. The attunement energies will flow through the Reiki Master and into the student. These special energies are guided by the Higher Power and make adjustments in the students energy pathways and connect the student to the source of Reiki. Because the energetic aspect of the attunement is guided by the Higher Power, it adjusts itself to be exactly right for each student. During the attunement, some students feel warmth in the hands, others may see colors or have visions of spiritual beings. However, it is not necessary to have an inner experience for the attunement to have worked. Most simply feel more relaxed.

Q. Can I treat myself?

A. Yes, once you have received the attunement, you can treat yourself as well as others. This is one of the unique features of Reiki.

Q. I have heard that Reiki can be sent to others at a distance. How does this work?

A. Yes, in Reiki II, you are given three Reiki symbols. These symbols are empowered by the Reiki II attunement. One of these symbols is for distant healing. By using a picture of the person you would like to send Reiki to or by writing the person's name on a piece of paper or simply by thinking of the person and also activating the distant symbol, you can send Reiki to them no matter where they are. They could be hundreds of miles away, but it makes no difference. The Reiki energy will go to them and treat them. You can also send Reiki to crisis situations or world leaders and the Reiki energy will help them too.

Q. How many levels are there to the Reiki training?
A. In the Usui/Tibetan system of Reiki taught by the Center, there are four levels. These include one, two, Advanced and Master.

Q. What does it feel like to give a treatment?
A. When giving a Reiki treatment, the Reiki energy flows through the practitioner before leaving the hands and flowing into the client. Because of this, the practitioner receives a treatment also. As the Reiki energy flows through the practitioner, she/he will feel more relaxed and uplifted. Spiritual experiences sometimes take place. The practitioner sometimes receives insights about what the client needs to know to heal more deeply.

Q. How do I find a Reiki teacher that is right for me?
A. Reiki teachers or Masters advertise in many magazines and also post notices at health food stores, new age bookstores and other places. Once you find a Reiki teacher or practitioner you are interested in receiving training or a treatment from, it is a good idea to ask them some important questions. Here are a few that will give you additional information to make a choice.

- How long have you been working with Reiki? What training have you had? How often do you teach? How do you personally use Reiki? What is your lineage?

- What qualifications are required to take Reiki Training?

- What do you cover in your classes? How many hours of class time is included? How much time is instructional, and how much is hands on practice?
- What are the specific things I will be able to do after taking the training?
- What are your fees, and will I get a certificate and a manual?
- Can I take notes and tape record the class?
- How many symbols will I learn?
- Is there a Reiki support group in my area or can you help me establish one?
- Will you openly support me in being a successful Reiki practitioner or Master?
- Do you have a positive respectful attitude toward other Reiki practitioners and Masters regardless of lineage or affiliation?

Be aware of how you feel about their answers and if they are responding in a loving manner that is supportive and empowering. Listen to your heart and you will be guided to the right teacher or practitioner.

Q. Can children learn Reiki?
A. Yes, Reiki can be taught to anyone. I recommend that a child be old enough to understand what Reiki is and that the child request to receive Reiki.

Q. Is it safe for pregnant woman?
A. Since Reiki is guided by the Higher Power, the Reiki energy will know the condition of the client or student and adjust appropriately. Reiki can only do good. Many pregnant women have received treatments with great benefit to them and their unborn child. It has also been used during child birth. Pregnant women have also taken the Reiki training and received the Reiki attunement with beneficial results.

Q. What about babies?
A. Babies love Reiki. It is very healthy for them. Do not worry about it being too strong. Reiki automatically adjusts to what the baby needs.

Q. Can I treat animals or plants?
A. Animals love Reiki too. They seem to have a natural understanding of what Reiki is and its benefits. Once a pet has received a Reiki treatment, they will often let you know that they want more. Plants also respond well to Reiki.

Q. Are there any side effects from a Reiki treatment?
A. Most of the time a person will feel relaxed and uplifted by a Reiki treatment. However, sometimes a person will have what is called a healing crisis. As a person's vibration goes up, toxins that have been stored in the body will be released into the blood stream to be filtered by the liver and kidneys and removed from the system. When this happens, sometimes a person can get a headache or stomach ache or feel weak. If this happens, it is a good idea to drink more water, eat lighter meals and get more rest. The body is cleansing as part of the healing process so this is a good sign.

Q. Can it be used to help groups of people or even global crises?
A. Yes, this is one of the wonderful benefits of Reiki and is why it is such a wonderful technique for the new millennium. It allows individuals and groups to do something positive about the challenging situations we see on the news involving so many people all over the planet. Reiki can be used to reduce suffering and help people any where in the world. On our Reiki web site at www.reiki.org we list major world events to send Reiki to. As more and more people send Reiki to help the world heal, we will move quickly to a world of peace and harmony.

Q. How much does a treatment usually cost?
A. A Reiki treatment usually will cost between $25.00 and $100.00 depending on the area of the country. However, some practitioners offer treatments free of charge or for a donation.

Q. Can a person make a living from Reiki?
A. Yes, if you put your heart into it, you can develop a Reiki practice combined with teaching classes that can bring a regular income. This is a very fulfilling way to earn a living. See the chapter on Developing Your Reiki Practice on page 36.

Q. Can one become Licensed to practice and teach Reiki?
A. There are no governmental licensing programs at this time. However, the Center does have a licensing program for Reiki teachers. Please see page 151 for more details or request our Center Licensed Teachers Guidebook from the Center.

Q. Does insurance cover Reiki treatments?
A. Reiki is just starting to be recognized by insurance companies. While not many are covering Reiki treatments, some are. Check with your local insurance company for details.

Q. Can nurses or massage therapists get CEU credit for taking Reiki classes?
A. Classes taught by our Center Licensed Reiki teachers are approved to give CEU credits to nurses, massage therapists and athletic trainers.

Q. Are there any scientific experiments that demonstrate Reiki works?
A. Yes, see the chapter on Reiki research on page 67.

Q. Can you get more than one attunement?
A. Once you receive a Reiki attunement will last your whole life. However, if you get additional attunements for the same level, it will act to refine and strengthen your Reiki energy.

Q. What is lineage?
A. Reiki is a technique that is passed on from teacher to student over and over. If one has Reiki, than she/he will be part of a secession of teachers leading back to the founder of the system of Reiki one is practicing. In the case of Usui Reiki, the lineage would lead back to Dr. Usui.

The Usui Reiki Symbols

Usui Reiki symbols are sacred and are to be kept confidential. They are only revealed to those who are about to be initiated into the Second or Third degree of Reiki. The reason for this is explained later in this article. However, it is possible to discuss their nature, how they work and their history while we continue to honor this trust.

Reiki symbols are an important and very interesting part of Reiki practice. They allow one to focus the energy of Reiki for specific purposes. (For a detailed explanation of what the symbols can be used for, see the book, "Reiki, The Healing Touch," or the audio cassette tape set, "The Reiki Class" available at the back of this book.) There are a total of four symbols in the Usui system of Reiki. Three are given in Reiki II and one in Reiki III. There are other symbols that people are using, but they are not a part of the Usui system.

Usui Reiki symbols are not as mysterious as they might seem. They are actually Japanese kanji which means they are simply words from the Japanese language. Their names can be found in a Japanese/English dictionary. The first two symbols vary from this somewhat. While the names of the Power and Mental/Emotional symbols are Japanese, the symbols themselves may be shamanic or a combination of Sanskrit and Japanese kanji. It is a practice of Japanese Buddhists' to sometimes combine ancient Sanskrit with Japanese kanji in their sacred writings and symbols so the way these first two symbols are drawn may have been influenced by this practice. In fact, our trip to Japan revealed that the mental/

emotional symbol likely came from the Sanskrit seed syllable *hrih* which the Tendai Buddhists call the love or harmony symbol. (See the chapter “Discovering the Roots of Reiki” on page 119 for more information on this.) The distant and Master symbols are completely Japanese kanji, both in their names and in the way they are drawn.

It is interesting to note that the name of the Usui Master symbol can be found in "The Encyclopedia of Eastern Philosophy and Religion" and is translated to mean "treasure house of the great beaming light." It is said to be, "a Zen expression for one's own true nature or Buddha-nature of which one becomes cognizant in the experience of enlightenment or satori." This is quite a profound definition. Perhaps it is called the Master symbol because it gives us direct connection to the Master within which is the real source of Reiki.

It is always important to know where a person's ideas are coming from. There are so many new Masters who are distantly removed in their lineage from Mrs. Takata and there have also been many changes and additions to Reiki with several new "branches" being added that it is apparent that in some cases the information being passed on has become confused. The information for this article comes from the training I received starting in 1981 from four Reiki Masters who received their Masterships directly from Mrs. Takata, plus my continuing research into Reiki including the exchange of symbols, attunements and important Reiki information with Reiki Masters from many lineages and backgrounds. I also received valuable information and confirmation of previous research from my trip to Japan in the fall of 1997.

The above information indicates that the Usui Reiki symbols are not exclusive to Usui Reiki. They existed prior to Dr. Usui's use of them. Also, because they are Japanese, it is not likely that he discovered them in a Sanskrit sutra as some have thought. It is much more likely that Dr. Usui received the symbols in his mystical experience on Mt. Kurama, or that he had prior knowledge of them from the Tendai Buddhists he was staying with. Since the symbols are Japanese and we know that the Master symbol is from Zen Buddhism, perhaps the sutra in which he discovered the formula for healing was Zen Buddhist rather than a Sanskrit sutra. (Even though there is a Sanskrit sutra that contains a formula for healing.) In addition, the Usui Master symbol also appears as part of the symbol on the Goshintai, which is the sacred scroll of the Johrei Fellowship. These are all interesting ideas to contemplate.

The Reiki symbols are transcendental in their functioning. Whereas most symbols have an affect on the subconscious mind of the user, causing a change in one's internal state, the Reiki symbols access the source of Reiki directly and signal a change in how the Reiki energy functions, independent of one's internal state. There are many ways to activate the Reiki symbols. They can be activated by drawing them with the hand, by visualizing them, or by saying the name either out loud or to oneself. Intention is the main ingredient in activation and it is possible with awareness to activate them by intention alone.

The power and effectiveness of the symbols comes from the Reiki attunement that is given during a Reiki class. Before the attunement, the student is shown the symbols and given time to memorize them. During the attunement, the energies of each symbol come down and enter the student's mind/body, linking themselves to the appropriate symbol in the student's mind. Afterward, whenever the student uses the symbol, the same energies they were linked to during the attunement are activated and begin flowing. This linking or activation of the Reiki symbols during the attunement process makes use of the stimulus/response mechanism which is a dynamic part of the human mind. The Reiki symbol becomes the stimulus and the particular energy the symbol represents is the response. However, because the attunement is guided by the Higher Power, and functions at a higher level of awareness, the stimulus/response mechanism doesn't require the repetition normally necessary to establish a relationship between stimulus and response. It happens immediately.

The Reiki symbols have traditionally been kept secret. While secrecy is a way of honoring their sacredness, there are also metaphysical reasons for this. One of the benefits of keeping the symbols secret until just before the attunement is to prevent the student from inadvertently linking the symbol to anything else but the energies they represent. If a student becomes aware of the Reiki symbols before a Reiki class, it is possible that energies of a lower vibration could connect to the symbol and possibly reduce the value of its use. Since the symbols have no real power without the attunement, it is better that they be kept secret until the class. In addition, if a person is shown a Reiki symbol without the benefit of the attunement that empowers it, they may incorrectly believe they have Reiki and not bother to take a class, thus missing the real experience of Reiki and losing the benefit of its healing power.

Many have noticed differences in the way the symbols are drawn when compared to the symbols from other Reiki Masters. These differences are there for a number of reasons. First, it is known that Mrs. Takata did not always draw the symbols exactly the same for every student she taught. After her transition, there was a meeting of the Reiki Masters she initiated. At the meeting they compared their symbols. The Power symbols of all the Masters present were basically the same. The Mental/Emotional symbols of the Masters had some slight differences. However, the Distant symbols were quite different - especially with the strokes at the bottom. They did not compare their Master symbols. So, even at this early date, there were differences which apparently came from Mrs. Takata. Perhaps she deliberately drew them differently to give a little distinction for each student or perhaps at other times, because of age or from having taught for over 30 years, she accidently drew them with some differences.

Also, there are different ways to draw the Japanese kanji figures and in fact, Mrs. Takata did have two ways she drew the Master symbol. One way was more of a cursive or flowing style, especially with the bottom part of the symbol. The other way she drew the Master symbol was in a printed or block style. (Both ways of drawing the Master symbol have exactly the same meaning.)

So starting out there were already changes in the symbols from one student to another. Add to this the fact that students were not allowed to make copies of the symbols, and had to keep them only in the mind. When it came time to pass them on, the teachers had to draw them from memory and since few people have perfect memories, some changes were bound to occur. This process has continued over and over thus allowing more changes to take place.

What is surprising is that for most students, the symbols still look fairly close to the original.

So, the question arises about whether there is a perfect or correct way to draw the symbols. From the above example, it can be seen that even those who learned from Mrs. Takata did not draw the symbols in exactly the same way - so there must not be a perfect way to draw them. It has also been found that everyone who has received the attunement for the symbols has symbols that work. So, the power of the symbols does not come from drawing them perfectly. It comes from the link that is made between the symbol the student receives in class and the attunement energies entering the student during the Reiki initiation. The correct way to draw the symbols is the way your Reiki Master drew them for you before you received the attunement. It is the link between the symbol and the Reiki energy that takes place during the attunement that empowers the symbols. The symbols that you received from your Master are the right symbols for you to use even if they are different than what others are using.

The Reiki symbols are a wonderful, beautiful way to connect to the higher power. Their use does not require that we be able to meditate or have years of spiritual practice. Their power and effectiveness comes to us by grace. which allows us to humbly accept the value we receive as a gift from the Creator. We are grateful for the efforts of Dr. Usui and all the others who have lovingly worked to make this system of healing available to us.

Are Your Usui Reiki Symbols Accurate?

Usui Reiki symbols have traditionally been kept secret. This has its value, but has also helped create a problem.

As the symbols were passed on orally from teacher to student over and over, the lack of a perfect memory on the part of the teachers and other problems allowed the symbols to change. In addition, some teachers channeled new symbols and began teaching them without telling their students they were non-Usui symbols. Because of this, some students are now receiving symbols that look nothing like the symbols taught by Dr. Usui. While it is true that all Reiki symbols work as long as they are empowered by a Reiki attunement, some students have expressed an interest in verifying the accuracy of their symbols. (The books currently published that include the symbols have not been thoroughly researched and may contain inaccuracies.)

If you have taken a Reiki II or Master class and wonder if you have received the original Usui Reiki symbols, send us a stamped self-addressed envelope and a copy of your Reiki certificate, and we will send you a copy of the original Usui Reiki symbols.

Strengthen Your Reiki Energy

The strength and value of the Reiki treatments you give can be improved by observing some simple guidelines. There are other things you can also do that will increase the strength of your Reiki. Remember, Reiki comes from an unlimited supply and contains the loving wisdom of the highest spiritual power. There is no limit to the benefit and value that is possible for you to receive from Reiki. As you try the techniques in this article, intend that they will work for you and know in your heart that this is right and you will get the improved results you seek.

The quality of the energy in the room you do your Reiki treatments in is important if improved results are what you seek. Make sure the room is not too hot or too cool. Make sure there is fresh air from an open window or that the room is not stuffy. A clean and orderly room is also helpful as negative psychic energy tends to collect around disorder and clutter. Smudge the room with sage before and after a treatment to release any negative energies left by past clients and to act as a blessing. As you smudge, call in the ancestors and the ascended masters and Reiki guides asking them to bless you and your client and to help you with your healing treatment. Place pictures of Dr. Usui, Dr. Hayashi, and Mrs. Takata around the room and ask them to be present also. The use of incense, essential oils or fresh flowers will also act to raise the vibration. Soothing music during the treatment will help the client move into a more receptive state of mind.

Before the client arrives, sit in a meditative state with your hands on your legs doing Reiki on yourself. Then after a few minutes, use your dominate hand to intently draw the Reiki Power symbol in light on each wall, and on the ceiling and floor. As you do this state "I bless this room with light" three times for each place. Then draw the power symbol in the center of the room and send Reiki into the room to fill the room with healing energy. You can also send distant Reiki to your client while they are on their way to the session so they will be relaxed and in a receptive state when they arrive.

Before starting the treatment, place the power and master symbols on your palm chakras. This will more completely open the palm chakras and energize them. Then draw a large power symbol down the front of your body to protect and empower you and draw smaller power symbols on each chakra. Placing the symbols into the clients crown chakra, and seeing them pass into the clients heart is also valuable before starting as it raises the vibration of the treatment and makes the energy of the symbols more available.

It is an interesting feature of Reiki that when giving a treatment, Reiki will continue to flow regardless of what you do with your mind. You can talk to others about any subject - including trivial matters, or gossip or even talk on the phone and Reiki will continue to flow and the client will receive some benefit. However, this sort of behavior does not produce the best results with Reiki. It must be kept in mind that giving Reiki is a spiritual experience and is more appropriately given with reverence. By meditating on the flow of Reiki as it passes through you, rather than talking, you will not only experience the energy more directly, but will also increase its flow. As you meditate on the Reiki energy, your mind merges with it and causes your energy field to resonate in greater harmony with the flow of Reiki, thus allowing it to flow more freely. As you do this, you may feel currents of energy flowing through various parts of your body including your spine, chakras, arms and hands. You may also feel heat, soothing sensations, vibrations, pulsations or waves of energy passing through you. By using your inner eye, you may also be able to see the Reiki energy. This may appear as tiny particles of white or golden light, or other colors of energy flowing through you. As you meditate and merge with these sensations, your mind will be uplifted, becoming more optimistic. Feelings of joy, peace and spiritual love will be experienced. Wonderfully positive fantasies and visions of higher spiritual planes can also be experienced.

By going inward and looking up through your crown chakra, it is even possible to psychically travel up to the source of Reiki and merge with it.

All these experiences are very enjoyable and can be deeply healing for the practitioner at the same time that they increase the benefit to the client. As you meditate on Reiki in this way, you will also be opening the pathways through which Reiki is able to flow, thus increasing the strength of Reiki you are channeling to your client. This is a very enjoyable way to improve the quality of the Reiki you give.

Adding prayer to your Reiki treatments is also an effective way to increase its strength. While you are giving a treatment, you can pray out loud or to yourself. Call on the ascended Reiki Masters, or on Jesus, St. Germain, Buddha, Krishna, Babaji, or other ascended masters, angels, or spirit guides, or pray directly to the infinite God/Goddess or to the Reiki energy itself. As you pray, ask that your Reiki be strengthened and ask it to bless you and your client. Ask it to bless and guide your Reiki practice and to guide you in increasing its strength and the benefit it provides you and those you treat. Accept the fact that there is no limit to the value and healing power that is available to you and ask that you be blessed with an abundance of healing, loving spiritual energy so that you will be of greater service to others. Combine your prayers with the above technique of merging with the energy and feeling it as it flows through you. By praying as you do Reiki, your prayers will be more powerful because when doing Reiki, you are more directly connected to the higher power which is the source of all answered prayer.

Attracting a special healing guide(s) that will work with you will also improve your treatments. While Reiki comes directly from God, there are spiritual guides who are adept at healing. They can add their Reiki energies to yours and also channel Reiki directly to the client. Many have reported that they felt additional hands on them and the presence of someone else in the room during a Reiki treatment. Having a sincere desire to help and praying that a healing guide or angel will come to help you can bring this about. Also, using the "Meet Your Reiki Guides" tape listed in the newsletter can create this connection.

Some Reiki practitioners report that their Reiki seems to have lost some of its power and they wonder why this happens and what can be done to get it back. It is a fact that when doing Reiki, the practitioner also receives a treatment. When this happens, sometimes negative energy is loosened and begins to move through the practitioners system on its way out. This energy can sometimes get stuck temporarily so that ones Reiki tends to work on the practitioner more than flowing to others. What is needed is for the practitioner to receive a treatment. This will release the blocked energy and restore the flow of Reiki. Remember, we need to maintain a balance of Reiki by treating ourselves, giving treatments to others and receiving treatments from others.

Your Reiki can also increase when you take your next level of Reiki training. The attunement for the next level and the use of the symbol(s) that go with it can definitely improve the quality of your Reiki treatments. This is regularly reported to occur by most students.

One practitioner reported that his wife was in continuous pain which was only partially and temporally removed with his Reiki II treatments. After taking the Master training, one treatment using the Master symbol completely released the pain and it didn't return.

Your Reiki can also improve by receiving additional attunements for the same level you already have. Even though you need only one attunement to have Reiki for the rest of your life, extra attunements for the same level you have will further refine and strengthen your Reiki. Many Masters will give extra attunements for free or for a low fee. Sometimes new Masters need people to practice on, go ahead and volunteer. A group of Masters can practice attunements on each other and strengthen their Reiki at the same time. Have each Master give the Master attunement to each person in the group. If you have five Masters, then each will receive four Master attunements and give four. This can be very powerful.

Chi Gong and Tai Chi are methods of developing your Chi and opening the pathways that Chi or Ki flows through. The pathways that are opened in these exercises are the same ones that Reiki flows through. On the average, most people who have practiced this type of moving meditation have stronger Reiki than those who have not. Find a teacher you feel comfortable with and take up the regular practice of Chi Gong or Tai Chi and not only will it be healthy for you, but your Reiki will also improve.

It is possible to use self-hypnosis and meditation as well as affirmations to improve your Reiki. Simply enter self-hypnosis or meditation and suggest to yourself that your Reiki is getting stronger and stronger and stronger and it will. You can also do this while giving a treatment.

Playing the "Chanting Reiki Masters" tape while give a treatment can also improve the value of your Reiki. The tape was made by 18 Reiki Masters who chanted the names of all four Reiki symbols into a microphone while intending that all who hear the sound will be healed. Most who play the tape while giving a treatment notice an improvement in the quality of their Reiki.

Placing sacred pictures in your Reiki room when you are doing Reiki can also increase the value of your treatments. This includes pictures of Jesus, Buddha, Krishna or any other spiritual teacher or great being. The Beaming Reiki Masters picture in the back of "Reiki, The Healing Touch" will also raise the vibration of your treatments as well as the Antakarana that is given in the Master training. You can place these cards under your Reiki table or on the wall of your healing room.

These are a few methods of improving the strength of your Reiki. Try them. Also remember that Reiki has it's own consciousness and by simply intending to find ways to improve the value you pass on to others with your treatments, and by being open to its guidance, the Reiki energy will guide you to additional ways. Reiki comes from an infinite supply. There is no limit to the healing power that is available to you. Focus on love and compassion. Trust in your inner guidance and take action on it. You will not be disappointed.

Developing Your Reiki Practice

Reiki is a truly wonderful gift and while some take Reiki training to use on themselves and with friends and family, many feel inspired to share it with a much wider circle. The development of a Reiki practice can be a very rewarding experience. Not only can it provide you with a source of income, there are spiritual experiences that can be much more meaningful. So, assuming you have been initiated into Reiki and have the ability to channel Reiki healing energy to others, I would like to share some ideas and techniques that may be helpful in developing a Reiki practice.

The most important thing concerning the development of a Reiki practice is the quality and strength of your intention. The mind is like a magnet. The quality and strength of your thoughts will determine the quality and strength of what you attract into your life. Therefore it is important for you to develop and maintain a positive mental attitude about your Reiki practice.

Decide with clarity, determination and commitment that you are going to create a thriving Reiki practice. Decide that you are worthy to do this and that there are many people who will benefit from your service. Decide that the value you and your clients will receive from your Reiki practice will far out weigh any effort or sacrifice that might be involved in creating it. Picture in your mind the results you want to create and how it will feel when you are actively involved in a thriving Reiki practice. Meditate frequently on this image and these feelings.

The Promise of a Developing Reiki Practice

People coming to you with many different problems, difficulties and illnesses sometimes as a last resort. Watching them leave relaxed, often radiant with joy and new hope. Seeing them improve over time, watching them grow, gain confidence and become more trusting of life. Seeing some make major changes and life adjustments. Occasionally witnessing miracles. Feeling the wonder of God's love pass through you and into another. Sensing the presence of spiritual beings, feeling their touch, knowing they work with you. Being raised into ever greater levels of joy and peace by simply placing your hands on another. Watching your life grow and develop as your continual immersion in Reiki transforms your attitudes, values and beliefs. Sensing that because of your commitment to help others, beings of light are focusing their love and healing on you and carefully guiding you on your spiritual path. This is the promise of a developing Reiki practice.

Allow them to fill you up and surround you and reach out to others. Use this to motivate you and to help you continue on in the face of doubt or discouragement. Know in your heart that the freedom, joy and satisfaction of having your own Reiki practice is a valid goal and that you are creating it. Believe in yourself and in your purpose.

If doubts arise about your goal, know that this is normal and assume that they have entered your consciousness because they are passing out of you. Whenever we take on a new level of healing or commit to a new goal, old negative thoughts and feelings that have been stored inside and have gone unchallenged are dislodged and begin moving through our consciousness. If your commitment is strong, these old negative feelings and thoughts will break up and be released. If you feel negative feelings and thoughts come up, know that this is part of your healing and that you are releasing them up to the Higher Power to be healed. Use your Reiki to speed this up and make sure to ask for treatments from others. Reiki psychic surgery can be especially helpful.

There are higher sources of help you can call on. Angels, beings of light and Reiki spirit guides as well as your own enlightened self are available to help you. They can help you develop your Reiki practice by directing clients to you and assisting with treatments. They can be of great benefit, but you must have a strong spiritual intention for your work if you are to recruit their aid. If you are doing Reiki in a selfish way, only for money or to gain control over others or to take on an air of self-importance, or for any other negative purpose, then it will be very difficult for these spiritual beings to work with you.

There must be congruence, an alignment within you in order for the Higher Power in the form of Reiki to flow through you in a powerful way and in order for the angels, Reiki spirit guides and other spiritual beings to work with you. Reiki wants only the best for you, but you must align with the nature of Reiki if you are to gain the greatest benefit. The more you can open to the true nature of Reiki which is to have an unselfish, heart centered desire to help others, then the more the Reiki spirit guides can help you.

Focus on helping others and on healing anything within yourself that may stand in the way of an uninhibited flow of love and compassion. This is what will make your Reiki practice a success!

The development of a spiritual attitude toward your Reiki practice can be facilitated through the regular use of affirmations and prayers. Try the following prayer: "Guide me and heal me so that I can be of greater service to others." By sincerely saying a prayer such as this each day, your heart will open and a path will be created to receive the help of higher spiritual beings. They will guide you in your Reiki practice and in the development of your life purpose.

One thing that can get in the way of developing a spiritual attitude about your Reiki practice is fear of competition. This has caused more problems and created more restrictions and negative energy in the Reiki community than any other area of misunderstanding. Lack is an illusion and this is especially true for Reiki! There is a far greater need for healing on the planet than there are Reiki practitioners who can provide it. Fear of competition goes directly against the nature of Reiki energy and because of this, it can repel people from you who might otherwise be interested in receiving a treatment. Reiki comes from an unlimited supply and does not fear competition. People who do Reiki together find that their Reiki gets stronger as more people join the group. If Reiki was competitive, then just the opposite would happen, it would be strongest when you were alone and get weaker as more people joined the group.

The nature of Reiki energy is one of cooperation. It understands the concept that we are all one and flows freely to anyone and everyone. It works in harmony with all other forms of treatment. It is clearly apparent, the wisdom of Reiki is to welcome all other practitioners as allies. If the spiritual purpose for your Reiki practice, is to help others and to heal the planet, then you can only rejoice when you hear about another Reiki practitioner in your area as they are helping you fulfill your purpose. Accept the wisdom of Reiki as your own wisdom, that all others who practice Reiki are helping you. The more you can do this, the more your Reiki practice will thrive.

Don't worry about taking clients away from other practitioners. Each practitioner has their own value and special way of helping others. You will attract the clients who are right for you. Others will attract the clients who are right for them.

An important trend is developing in society that will soon create a great demand for Reiki practitioners. More and more people are discovering the value of alternative therapy. A recent study conducted by Dr. David M. Eisenberg of Boston's Beth Israel Hospital indicates that people in the US are beginning to turn away from modern medicine and make greater use of alternative health care techniques. The survey concluded that 34 percent of Americans said they used at least one alternative therapy in 1990 and that Americans are spending nearly $14 billion a year for this treatment, most of which comes out of the patients own pocket. The therapies most used are meditation, touch therapy (such as Reiki), guided imagery, spiritual healing, chiropractic, hypnosis, homeopathy, acupuncture, herbal cures, and folk remedies.

Also of note is the fact that the National Institutes of Health has created an Office of Alternative Medicine whose purpose is to research alternative healing methods and establish their value. Already many healing techniques formerly considered quackery by the medical establishment have been proven valid by this new office. These include chiropractic, acupuncture and homeopathy and they will soon be studying touch therapy and Reiki. Clearly, a paradigm shift is taking place toward the general acceptance of alternative medical treatment. It is likely that Reiki will become widely accepted as a valid form of healing before the end of the decade! Think what this means for anyone with a Reiki practice. A great need is developing for Reiki practitioners!

Now that we have covered some of the important attitudes, values and beliefs necessary for a thriving Reiki practice, let's discuss some of the practical issues. An important issue is money. Some practitioners do not charge money and this is fine if that is their decision as everyone has the right to charge whatever they want or to charge nothing at all. However, it is often better for the client if they are able to give something in return. They are not paying for the Reiki energy which is free but for your time and the effort you have put forth to learn Reiki. When people receive a treatment for free they often feel indebted to the practitioner and guilty feelings can develop. This creates an imbalance that can get in the way of continued treatments. Charging money allows people the freedom to come whenever they want. If you do have clients who have a money problem, you can charge them less or barter.

How much should you charge for a Reiki session? A good rule of thumb is to charge about the same for a standard Reiki session as others in your area are charging for massage. A standard Reiki session will usually last about 45 minutes to an hour and a half.

When you first start charging for your sessions, you can start at a lower rate if that feels comfortable to you and increase it as your confidence and reputation grow.

Business cards are a good first step when starting your practice. They let people know you are serious about your Reiki business and make it easy for you to give people your phone number in case they want to make an appointment. It is not a good idea to place you address on the card as people may come without calling you. It is a good idea to talk to people first to get a feel for their energy, and let them know what they can expect from a Reiki session before setting up an appointment and giving them directions to your home or office.

Flyers are also a good idea. In your flyer explain what Reiki is and the benefits it offers along with your name and phone number. You can place them on bulletin boards in health food stores and new age book stores, etc. and they can be given out to prospective clients.

Beginning your Reiki practice from your home is a good idea as it will save money on start-up costs, but many practitioners have found advantages to having their own office. An office creates a professional atmosphere and lets people know that you take your work seriously. You may want to start in your home and get an office after things get going or if you can afford it, get an office right away. Consider the fact that you may want to have group activities in your office when considering the size office you want.

Make sure to get each clients name address and phone number for your mailing list. As your list grows, you can mail out flyers on up-coming Reiki events or simply remind people about your practice. A good way to keep track of your clients is to use a client information form. The one in the back of "Reiki, The Healing Touch" is a good one as it includes a disclaimer which protects you from misunderstandings about the results you promise from a Reiki session. Feel free to make copies of this form and use it in your practice. Keep your mind open to other ways of adding people with an interest in alternative healing to your mailing list. The mailing list can be an important tool in promoting your Reiki practice.

One way to let people know about your Reiki practice is to offer to exchange Reiki with other alternative therapists. This works well with massage therapists as they are familiar with body work and often need therapy themselves. Offer to refer clients to them and ask them to do the same for you. Give them some of your flyers or business cards to display in their office.

When you are at public gatherings or around others and someone complains about an ache or pain, offer to give them Reiki. If they have never heard of Reiki before, explain that it is a Japanese form of stress reduction with many healthy benefits. If they have a metaphysical understanding you can talk about Ki and the life force, etc. Talk to them on a level they can understand. Take 15 minutes or so to treat the area of concern and let them know you do this professionally and give them your card. Tell them what a complete session is like and set up an appointment if they are interested. At parties or large gatherings, the attention you attract when giving Reiki to one often creates interest in others who will want a sample treatment also. Often you end up treating several people and passing out many business cards. As you treat you can talk about Reiki and how it works. Ask the person to explain what they feel. This always creates a lot of interest. Being focused on helping the person and not on getting a client is the key to attracting people for sample treatments. However, if they are interested, a business card is appropriate.

One thing that will really attract attention for your Reiki practice is wearing a Reiki T-shirt. People will want to know what the symbols mean and this opens the door to talking about Reiki. Offer to give them a sample treatment and tell them about your practice. If they seem interested, give them a business card and if possible, set up an appointment.

A free Reiki evening can create lots of interest. Plan one night a month to talk about Reiki and give sample treatments. If you have Reiki friends, ask them to come and help give treatments. This is a great way to help others and let them know about Reiki and your practice. Make up flyers for your free Reiki evening and put them up in appropriate places. If the Reiki practitioners can meet an hour or so before the meeting to give treatments to each other it will really improve the quality of what the non-Reiki people receive. Also, if you have taken Reiki III/Master training, you could give a refresher attunement or healing attunement to each of the practitioners to boost their energy. This is a great way for the practitioners to practice their Reiki and for you to practice giving attunements. Call everyone you know who would be interested and let them know.

If your area has psychic or wholistic fairs, get a booth. Take a Reiki table and ask five or more of your Reiki friends to help.

Offer 10 or 15 minute treatments with five or more Reiki practitioners giving a treatment to one person at a time. Charge $10.00 or so per treatment. This can be a powerful healing experience and a good demonstration of Reiki. Have a table with your flyers and business cards on it and be sure to get each persons name, address, and phone number for your mailing list. Another way is to use chairs and have one or two practitioners give 10 or 15 minute treatments to each person. The chair method takes up less space and allows you to treat more than one person at a time.

Create a healing service at your church. Recruit other healers to help. You could use both Reiki and non-Reiki healers. This can create tremendous interest in Reiki. Refer to the Summer 93 issue of the *Reiki News* for a complete explanation.

Volunteer to do free Reiki treatments at hospitals, hospice centers, drug and alcohol treatment centers or in conjunction with a psychologist or other therapists. By doing this, you will gain experience and people will find out about your practice, but most of all, you will be helping others.

If there is a metaphysical/wholistic paper in your area, offer to write an article for it on Reiki or healing in general. Make sure your name and phone number are listed and that you are a Reiki practitioner or teacher. If you are really serious, decide to write an article every month. This will let people know who you are and what your attitudes and beliefs are concerning healing. They will then be able to decide if they want to come to you. It is also a good idea to place an ad in the same paper your article appears in. You will pay for the ad, but the article will be free!

Write articles for the *Reiki News* or send in a description of your Reiki experiences. The *Reiki News* needs articles and is very interested in letting people know about your personal experiences with Reiki. It goes out to over 60,000 people interested in Reiki all over the US and other countries. Having your name in the paper will improve your reputation especially if you place free copies in your local health and new age book stores and hand out copies to your clients and friends, etc.

Develop a Reiki talk and offer to speak about Reiki to local groups. There are many groups looking for speakers and alternative healing is becoming a hot topic. If you have little experience at public speaking, you can join a local Toast Masters Club. There you will be coached and given ample opportunity to develop your speaking ability. If you are making Reiki your career, then the ability to speak before groups is a must. Decide to become a great speaker and go for it.

In many parts of the country the news media are reporting the positive benefits of alternative healing. So, call the local newspapers and TV stations. Find out which reporter(s) are in charge of or interested in information about alternative healing. Talk to them and let them know you are a Reiki practitioner/teacher. Explain Reiki to them in a way they can understand - tell them it is a Japanese form of stress reduction and relaxation that can also facilitate healing. Tell them there are over 1,000,000 practitioners in the US and the numbers are growing! Give them details and make it interesting and exciting. Offer to give them a free treatment. Let them know that you are available should they decide to write an article or air a program about Reiki or alternative healing or if any questions come up about it in the future. Establish in their mind that you are an expert on Reiki. They will then think of you as a resource person. Most reporters keep a file of people they can call on for different subjects and they will probably put your name in it! If they are not ready to do a story now, when they are ready, it is likely they will call you!

Become Licensed as a Reiki Master/Teacher by the Center. When you do this, we will list your classes in the newsletter and refer students and clients to you. The Center continually receives requests from people from all over the country who are interested in Reiki sessions and classes. If you are Licensed by the Center, we can then refer these prospective clients to you.

If you are beginning to teach and are having trouble getting a class together, simply plan a class, set a date and assume the class will be full. Then when you tell people about the class, they will pickup a positive attitude from you about the class and want to come. If people sense a tentativeness, it will discourage them from attending. Being decisive about your plans and having a positive attitude will attract students and bring the class together. Your guides will also be better able to work with you if you are clear about what you intend to do.

These ideas have worked for others, they will work for you. Try them! Also, use your intuition to develop other ways to promote your Reiki practice. Remember, a clear intension is the first step to success. Keep track of the result you get with each thing you try. Keep using the ones that work and drop the ones that don't. Keep trying new things until you get the results you want. By following this formula you will create a successful Reiki practice and in so doing, bring joy, peace and healing to others.

Becoming a Reiki Master

Reiki is a sacred practice that requires reverence and our greatest respect if we are to experience its most wonderful value. The benefits of Reiki can be all encompassing, not only giving us the ability to heal ourselves and others, which by itself is deeply meaningful, but also bringing guidance for our lives. Its unlimited nature can create opportunities for continual growth, unfoldment and the awakening of our own boundless potential. The ever increasing joy, peace and abundance that await those who sincerely pursue the path of Reiki are not only a blessing to be enjoyed, but also contain the healing that the planet so dearly needs. Those who have been initiated into Reiki often feel this greater potential and aspire to continue on to the Advanced and Master levels.

The desire to grow is inherent in simply being alive. As we look around ourselves and observe living things, we can clearly see that the one activity all living things share is growth. Everything that is alive grows. Because this is what living things do, one could even say that the purpose of life is to grow. Therefore, the desire to grow in ones Reiki potential is a natural expression of ones core essence and of life itself. If you feel this desire in your heart, honor and respect it. Doing so, will fulfill an innate need.

The joys of becoming a Reiki Master are many and you don't necessarily have to teach in order for the Master training to be useful. The additional healing energy, symbols, techniques and knowledge will add value to your healing abilities. Treating yourself, giving yourself and others healing attunements and treating others in person and at a distance will all be noticeably improved. The fact that you can pass Reiki on to friends and family is also a definite plus. Many take the Master training with just this in mind. However, if you ever decide to formally teach, you will be able to do so. As each person takes the Reiki Master training, and increases their personal vibration, this adds to the vibration of the whole planet!

One of the greatest joys of Reiki Mastership is teaching Reiki to others. Imagine the thrill of witnessing the members of your Reiki class receiving Reiki energy during the attunement. Then, as you guide them in its use, sharing in their joy and amazement as they experience it's gentle power flowing though them for the first time. As your students use Reiki to help family, friends and clients, a wonderful sense of spiritual connection will develop between all of you. Feelings of compassion and love for everyone will be strengthened as you merge with the Reiki Consciousness and know more deeply that we come from God and that we are all one in God.

Much of the information about Reiki has come to us through Mrs. Takata who learned the system of Reiki in Japan in 1935. According to Mrs. Takata, the definition of a Reiki Master is anyone who has received the Master attunement and Master symbol, understands how to give all the attunements and has actually taught a Reiki class thus passing Reiki on to others. Those who have taken Reiki Master training and not taught at least one person would not qualify as Reiki Masters and should call themselves Reiki Master practitioners until they do teach. If you have taught a friend or family member, then you qualify as a Reiki Master.

After Mrs. Takata passed on in December, 1980, the twenty-two Masters she had initiated continued to teach and eventually began initiating other Masters. At first they taught in the same way Mrs. Takata had done, teaching the complete system in three degrees. Eventually some Masters began making changes to the system, adding knowledge and healing skills they had acquired from experience and inner guidance. Some took the third degree that originally contained the complete Master training and broke it up into two or more parts. Some actually broke the Master degree up into as many as five parts, calling each part a new degree.

When seeking a Reiki Master to take the Master training from, it is important to ask her/him exactly what you will be able to do after you take the Master training from them. Will you receive the complete training and be able to initiate others into all the degrees including full Reiki Master or will something be left out, requiring you to take additional sublevels or degrees and pay additional fees? Because of the changes some have made to the system of Reiki, this is a very important question.

Becoming a Reiki Master is a serious step that must be preceded by necessary preparation. One must first take Reiki I & II and Advanced Reiki training. It is also necessary to meditate on your life purpose and decide if Reiki Mastership is in harmony with it. Then, it is important to find a Reiki Master to study with who is competent and who you feel attuned to and will support you after you become a Reiki Master.

Becoming a Reiki Master implies that you will be able to initiate others into Reiki. Therefore, it is important to find a teacher who will spend time in class helping you practice the attunement process. Ask your teacher how much time is spent in class practicing the attunements as some teachers spend little or none. Also ask them how much support they are willing to give you to begin teaching your own classes. This is important. Some Reiki Masters will have little interest in helping you get started as they are afraid you will take student away from them. If you are serious about becoming a successful teaching Reiki Master, find a teacher who will openly support you in achieving your goal.

Before teaching your first class, additional practice doing the attunements is a good idea. This can be done on friends who already have Reiki. Ask them if they would like to be an "attunement model" and let them know that the additional attunements will be beneficial for them and will refine and strengthen their Reiki energies. Most will gladly agree. If you can't find someone to practice on, you can use a teddy bear or a pillow to represent a person.

It will also be necessary to practice the talks, lectures and meditations you will be leading in class. Make outlines of your talks and practice into a tape recorder. Listen to your tapes and take notes on ways you can improve your talks. Then continue to practice until you are confident. Don't be afraid to use your outline in class. When teaching, relax and let the Reiki energy do the work.

If you have a sincere desire to help others and have taken the time to prepare to teach, you should have no trouble attracting students. It is your attitude that creates the results you receive so, assume success and you will create success. (See the previous two articles for ideas on promoting your practice.)

As a teaching Reiki Master it is important to treat your students with the greatest respect. Know that each has the spark of God within them. Never use subtle threats or the withholding of information to cause your students to be dependent on you. Openly encourage each student to be connected to her/his own power and freedom of choice. What you create for others comes back to you. As you truly empower others, so will you be empowered. Trust in the abundance of the universe and you will receive abundance and you will also be blessed with peace and joy.

When teaching Reiki to others, it is important to set a good example by being an authentic representative of Reiki energy. People cannot be so easily fooled by surface spirituality now. They want and need a real teacher who comes from experience and is working on her/his own deep healing. This requires one to meditate on the nature of Reiki energy and surrender to it. It is a continual process of working with all aspects of ones being that are out of step with Reiki energy and allowing those aspects to be healed by Reiki energy. We must seek to develop and express the qualities of love, compassion, wisdom, justice, cooperation, humility, persistence, kindness, courage, strength, and abundance as Reiki energy is all of these and more. It may seem paradoxical, but it is true that a true Reiki Master is one who is always becoming a Reiki Master. Like life itself, it is a process of continual growth.

As you do this, you will realize sooner or later that there is more to Reiki than using it to heal yourself and others of specific problems. Reiki has a deeper purpose. In the same way that Reiki is able to guide healing energy when you are giving a treatment, Reiki can guide your life.

There is a perfect plan for your life that has always been present and has been waiting for you. This plan is exactly what is good and right and healthy for you. This plan is not based on what your parents want for you, or what the culture says you need to be accepted, but on what will really make you happy. This plan is inside you and comes from your core essence. Reiki can guide you to this plan and help you follow it. This plan is your true spiritual path.

By treating yourself and others and meditating on the essence of Reiki, you will be guided more and more by Reiki in making important decisions. Sometimes you will find yourself doing things that don't make sense or conform to what you think you should be doing and sometimes you will be guided to do things that you have vowed you would never do. However, by trusting more and more in the guidance of Reiki, by letting go of what your ego thinks it needs to be happy and by humbly surrendering to Reiki's loving power, you will find your life changing in ways that bring greater harmony and feelings of real happiness.

Over time, you will learn from experience that the guidance of Reiki is worthy of your trust. Once you have surrendered completely, you will have entered the Way of Reiki. When you do this, you will be at peace with the past and have complete faith in the future and know that there never was anything to worry about. Your life will work with ever greater harmony and you will feel that you have reached your goal of wholeness even as you continue to move toward it!

In the end, we must consider that a Reiki Master is not one who has mastered Reiki, but one who has been mastered by Reiki. This requires that we surrender completely to the spirit of Reiki, allowing it to guide every area of our lives and become our only focus and source of nurturing and sustenance. As we proceed toward the end of the millennium, the Way of Reiki offers itself as a solution to our problems and a path of unlimited potential. May all who would benefit from this path be guided to it.

Issues of Time and Money

One area of concern in the Reiki community is the period of time one should wait between Reiki classes. Center policy is that a person needs to decide within themselves when they are ready to continue with their Reiki training. While it is important for a student to practice what they have learned before going on, each student is different in their needs and in their capacity to absorb new information. Because of this, it is difficult to set a fixed time period between classes that is right for every student. That is why it is important for the Reiki student to develop and rely on their own inner guidance to determine when they are ready for the next level.

However, according to some Reiki Masters, there must be a fixed time between Reiki classes in order for the training to be effective and in order for it to qualify as Usui Reiki. The formula commonly promoted is three to six months between Reiki I & II and as much as three years between Reiki II and Master. It is implied that this is the way it has always been and that you must teach this way if you are teaching the Usui system. Otherwise, it is stated that your Reiki is not valid and it could result in problems in the use of Reiki.

The required waiting periods between classes was never part of the original Usui system. Information from members of the original Usui Shiki Reiki Ryoho in Japan indicates that a rigid method of training was not used and the amount of time between degrees varied between students. This also goes against how Mrs. Takata received her Reiki training. According to an interview that appeared in the Honolulu Advertiser in 1974, Mrs. Takata mastered the art of Reiki in one year. She did not have to wait three years to become a Reiki Master. It is also not how Mrs. Takata trained her Reiki students. In "Journey Into Consciousness" my first Reiki Master, Bethel Phaigh, explains that she learned the whole system of Reiki from Mrs. Takata in nine months and was given the Master level only a few days after receiving Reiki II. I have also received letters from several other Reiki students who knew Mrs. Takata personally and received their Reiki training from her who state that she had taught Reiki I & II together in just one day. Apparently Mrs. Takata treated each student according to what she/he needed and according to what was right for them as individuals. She had no set rules about how long one must wait between degrees.

The idea that you must wait a specific period of time between degrees is something that a few Reiki Masters added to the way they taught Reiki after Mrs. Takata passed on. It is not based on how she taught nor on how Reiki is taught by the original Usui group in Japan. Each Reiki Master has the right to decide how long her/his students need between classes or to allow each student to decide for themselves.

Another area of concern within the Reiki community is the fee that one should pay to become a Reiki Master. It is Center policy that a Reiki Master has the right to charge whatever fee she/he feels guided to charge or to charge no fee at all. We feel that this is something that must be decided by the Master using her/his inner guidance. Those that charge a high fee also have a right to do so. Also, because we feel that all actions a person takes on the spiritual path are right for them, those who pay a high fee are supposed to pay a high fee. The same is true for those who charge or pay low fees or no fee. The fee issue is an individual one and each person needs to look within themselves to decide how much they are willing to pay and how much to charge once one becomes a Reiki Master.

However, according to some Reiki Masters, a high fee, often stated to be $10,000 must be paid in order for your Reiki Mastership to be valid. It is implied that this fee has always been part of the Reiki program and was part of the information that Dr. Usui originally received. It is said by these same Masters that if you don't charge or pay this fee, then you are not a Master of the Usui system.

This "need" for a high fee is not based on any verifiable facts. The Reiki story told by Mrs. Takata indicates that Dr. Usui didn't pay anything for his Reiki training, having received it on a beam of light directly from the source.

There is also some question about what Mrs. Takata paid for her Mastership. In order for Mrs. Takata to go to Japan, prior to her knowing about Reiki, she had to sell her house in order to pay for her steamship ticket. This really has no bearing on what she paid for her Reiki training and it is not known how much Mrs. Takata paid for her Mastership or if she paid anything at all.

The idea of charging a $10,000 fee for Reiki Mastership was never a part of how Dr. Usui practiced Reiki. It was actually started in 1970 by Mrs. Takata when she initiated her first Reiki Master. She felt that because Reiki is so easily acquired, not needing years of discipline, but simply being passed on to the student through the Master, the western mind would have no respect for Reiki unless a high fee was charged. In Japan respect for authority is part of the culture and so a high fee was not necessary. Mrs. Takata began charging $10,000 for Reiki Mastership as an artificial way of creating respect. It must be understood that real respect for Reiki must come from appreciating the healing value it has and not from what one has paid for it.

Simply because Mrs. Takata was guided to charge this amount doesn't mean that all Reiki Masters should charge this amount. Experience has demonstrated that the quality of the Reiki energy one receives has no connection to the fee one pays. God does not respond to money, but to sincerity, humility and trust. There are those who have paid high fees and received poor training and there are those who have paid low fees and received excellent training.

The important thing here is not the fee you pay, but the quality of training you receive. Ask your prospective Reiki Master exactly what you will be receiving for your money. Also check with other students who have become Masters through them to see if they are happy with what they received and if they feel supported in becoming successful Reiki Masters.

While each Reiki Master has a right to charge whatever they want, it is important to realize that high fees often prevent people from becoming Reiki Masters. High fees for Mastership also invite problems of greed, power over others and elitism which go directly against the nature and purpose of Reiki healing energy. High fees for Mastership may have had some value in the past and may still have value for some teachers and students. However, times have changed. World population is growing and the planet is becoming overcrowded resulting in widespread suffering. We need as many Reiki Masters as possible so that the healing power of Reiki can be used to help solve our problems. While I respect the right of each Reiki Master to charge whatever they feel is right, I also think that high fees slow down the spread of Reiki unnecessarily and prolong suffering. Seeking to align with the purpose of Reiki energy, The International Center for Reiki Training has chosen fees that are more affordable and similar to fees charged for other types of training of similar value.

Fortunately, the issue of high fees is not as big a problem as it was in the 80's and early 90's. It is clear that the energy of Reiki itself has healed it's own expression. As we enter the new millennium, a more balanced way of teaching Reiki has developed.

Reiki and Legal Issues

Because Reiki is the practice of laying on hands for therapeutic purposes, there may be laws in your state governing its practice. There are also other legal considerations that need to be kept in mind when practicing Reiki. While I have never heard of anyone having a legal problem due to the practice of Reiki, it is good to be well informed so as to avoid the possibility of problems arising.

To make sure there is no misunderstanding about Reiki, it is important to let your clients know that Reiki is a laying on hands healing technique and that it is done without the person disrobing. Make sure they understand this and that they feel comfortable with you placing your hands on them. Explain the various hand positions and let them know if they feel uncomfortable about being touched, you can do the entire treatment without touching them by placing your hands three to four inches away from their body. When treating any sensitive areas such as the genitals or breasts, it is important to get permission to treat these areas first and then treat them with your hands away from the body. By doing this, you will avoid the issue of inappropriate touching.

It is also important to let your clients know you are not a doctor or psychologist (unless you are) and that the most you will guarantee is relaxation and stress reduction. It is important to let your clients know that while many people have received healing, you can't guarantee healing results (remember, doctors and psychologist don't guarantee results either) and if they do have a medical or psychological problem, you suggest they see an enlightened health care professional.

Never suggest they change or eliminate any medications they may have been placed on by their doctors. An easy way to do this is to use the "Client Information Form" in the back of "Reiki, The Healing Touch." (Note: while "Reiki, The Healing Touch" is copyrighted, you do have permission to make copies of this one page.) Have them read it and sign it. This way there will be no misunderstandings and little chance of any legal problems.

The Center is looking into making malpractice insurance available to Reiki practitioners. This can be important for anyone charging money for Reiki treatments. While few have had legal problems, it is always better to be prepared. Also, if you want to work in a doctors office or hospital, malpractice insurance is usually required. Please contact us if you are interested.

Some states or local areas have laws governing who can touch others for therapy. In some areas, you may be asked to get a massage license or in other areas, only doctors or nurses may be permitted to touch others for therapeutic reasons. Check with your local or state governments to see if there are any laws governing touch therapy. Let the government officials know that Reiki is not massage. Tell them it is energy work and you may find that no license is required. So far, this has not been an issue for Reiki practitioners, but situations are changing and it is prudent to be aware. Check with your state and local government and see if any legislation is being planned. If it is, it is important for you to be fully aware of what is being considered and then to make sure your best interests are being represented as a Reiki practitioner.

If legal concerns arise involving the touching aspect of Reiki, just remember, you can give an entire Reiki treatment without touching. This may be one way to avoid any problems. Another thing you can do is to become a minister in a church where laying on hands is part of their program. By doing this, Reiki becomes part of practicing your religion. Because of this, it can't be restricted or regulated by laws. There are many churches who list laying on hands as part of their ministry that will ordain you as a minister with little or no requirements. An added benefit of being a minister is you will be able to perform weddings. Here are two churches you might want to try: Universal Life Church, 601 Third St., Modesto, CA 95351, Phone (209) 527-8111. No charge. Registered in all states. Universal Church of the Master, 15602 Maubert Ave., San Leandro, CA 94578.

Reiki for Success

Inside every person there is a need to feel fulfilled, a need to do something worthwhile with our lives. We long to lead lives that are supportive of our well-being and that causes us to feel happy. This inner need can be a strong motivational force that causes many people to go to great lengths to achieve it. Yet the feeling of fulfillment that we seek is often sidetracked by the misguided influence of those around us. So often we accept goals that are given to us by our parents, our peers or by the culture claiming that if we achieve them, then we will be happy. We are often told that if we have the right job, drive the right car, have the right house in the right neighborhood, have the right clothes and friends, etc. then we will be happy. However, those that achieve these goals often end up not so happy and find themselves abusing alcohol, drugs, food, sex, money, power, etc. in a continuing but unsuccessful attempt to find happiness. So often, people choose their goals based on what will cause them to look good in the eyes of others. They are seeking the approved life style and when they have it, they often find their satisfaction to be shallow and short lived. They end up feeling empty and unfulfilled. The goals they sought did not bring the results they truly needed.

What is needed for real success is to look inside and see what you need and what you need to do as an individual to be happy. Often this will look completely different than what you were told you needed by your parents or friends or the culture. The next thing you must do is have the courage to base your goals on your inner needs, create plans to achieve them and act on those plans.

When we follow our inner guidance in this way, we are often asked to do things that are difficult for us to do. Often, we will not have the support of our parents, or friends or the culture. We may be told that what we are trying to do doesn't make any sense or that we will fail and be unhappy. Yet, we must continue to focus on our inner guidance and do what we need to do.

When I was in my 30's I had moved from Detroit to Hawaii. After living in Hawaii for over nine years I thought I really had it made. I was the envy of all my friends who were still living back in Detroit. The weather was beautiful and Hawaii was a wonderful place to be. Yet, when I looked inside, I found that I was not happy. My inner guidance told me that to fulfill my inner needs, I needed to move and by following my guidance, I ended up back in Detroit. This was a very difficult thing to do, yet when I got back to Detroit, things started to get better. There were many people and resources in Detroit that were exactly what I needed to heal and grow. The longer I stayed, the better things got and I knew deep inside that my inner needs were being fulfilled and that I was making real progress with the personal issues that I had neglected for so long. The longer I stayed, the better things got and to this day, things have not stopped getting better.

The thing that made the difference for me was Reiki. While living in Hawaii, I received Reiki training. After this, things began to change. Reiki strengthened my connection to my inner self. I also felt greater courage in facing personal challenges. I began treating myself with Reiki everyday and while doing so I said a prayer. The prayer is "Guide me and heal me so that I might be of greater service to others." I said this prayer sincerely and was ready to act on the guidance I received. By doing this, I was able to let go of my false self more and more and to face and deal with the areas in my life that needed to heal. The success I experienced with this process created a growing feeling of trust in the source - the source of Reiki, the source of all.

As I asked and received guidance and healing from Reiki, I realized that because Reiki comes from the "Higher Self" it always guides us to the goals that are just right for us as individuals. I found that often I was asked to do things that were difficult, yet as soon as I accepted the challenge, people and resources appeared in my life to help and the goal became easier to achieve than what I had thought it would be. As each goal was achieved, the new experiences I had gave me greater confidence in living my life, and in doing a wider range of things, thus my comfort zone expanded. As I continued this process over time I began to see a pattern of guidance and success that indicated a greater purpose. I found that Reiki was healing and guiding me ever closer to a way of life filled only with harmony, peace and success. As I meditated on this, it became apparent that Reiki can create a way of living, doing, and being just right for each individual that is filled with ever increasing happiness. I came to call this process "The Way of Reiki." "The Way of Reiki" is a spiritual path that is just right for each person. No matter what you have been doing with your life and no matter where you are, it is always possible for Reiki to lead you back to your true spiritual path. This is the wonderful nature of Reiki. It contains all the positive qualities one needs for personal development as well as the guidance necessary for one's spiritual path.

Here is a specific Reiki technique you can use to help achieve your goals. (Remember, because Reiki is guided by the Higher Power, it will only help you achieve goals that are in harmony with the divine plan.) If you are having trouble achieving a goal that you believe to be a worthy goal for yourself, accept that there may be a part of yourself that is resisting your success that needs to heal. Use the distant symbol and send Reiki to this part. Simply draw out the distant symbol and state "I now send Reiki to the part of myself that needs to heal in order for me to achieve (state your goal here). Hold your hands on your body or out in your aura intending for Reiki to flow to this part no matter where it might be. As the Reiki starts flowing, say a prayer calling on the Higher Power to heal this part and to show you any lesson(s) you might need to learn in order to achieve your goal.

If your goal truly is worthy, then healing will take place and/or you will be shown the lesson you need to learn to achieve your goal. If it is not a worthy goal, then you will be shown this also and how you need to change your goal or you may be given an alternative goal that is worthy. Use this technique as often as you need until you achieve your goal.

Reiki Research

Scientific research in the area of laying on hands has been conducted for many years. There are now quite a few experiments that validate the usefulness of Reiki and Reiki-like healing techniques. Some of the more interesting results of these experiments demonstrate that their positive results are coming from more than just the placebo effect, while others indicate the energy is non-physical in nature in that the benefits do not diminish regardless of the distance between sender and receiver. A new book by Daniel Benor, M.D. titled "Spiritual Healing, Does It Work, Research Says Yes" which is available from Vision Publications describes over 200 scientific studies in the area of Spiritual Healing, most of which show positive results. See page 158. The following are a few of the more interesting experiments.

Wetzel, a registered nurse describes a Reiki experiment she conducted in her paper, "Reiki Healing: A Physiologic Perspective." In her study, forty-eight people made up the experimental group while ten made up a control group. Both groups had blood samples taken at the beginning and at the end of the experiment. The experimental group received First Degree Reiki training. The control group was not involved in the Reiki training.

The blood samples were measured for hemoglobin and hematocrit values. Hemoglobin is the part of red blood cells that carry oxygen. Hematocrit is the ratio of red blood cells to total blood volume. The people in the experimental group who received Reiki training experienced a significant change in these values with 28 percent experiencing an increase and the remainder experiencing a decrease. The people in the control group who did not receive Reiki training experienced no significant change. It is thought that changes, whether an increase or decrease are consistent with the purpose of Reiki which is to bring balance on an individual basis.

One individual experienced a 20% increase in these values. She continued to treat herself with Reiki daily and after three months, her increase had been maintained and in fact had continued to improve. This improvement was appropriate for her as she had been experiencing iron deficiency anemia.

Another experiment using Therapeutic Touch, a technique which is similar to Reiki has also demonstrated its ability to increase hemoglobin values. Otelia Bengssten, M.D. conducted an experiment with a group of 79 sick patients. Together the patients had a wide range of diagnosed illnesses including pancreatitis, brain tumor, emphysema, multiple endocrine disorders, rheumatoid arthritis, and congestive heart failure. Laying-on hands treatments were given to 46 patients with 33 as controls. The treated patients showed significant increases in hemoglobin values. The effect was so pronounced that even cancer patients who were being treated with bone marrow-suppressive agents which predictably induce decreases in hemoglobin values showed an increase. The majority of patients also reported improvement or complete disappearance of symptoms. Both this experiment and the one above, demonstrate that healers are able to induce actual biological improvements in the patients they treat rather than simply create a feeling of well-being.

Laying-on hands healing has been validated by experiments carried out at St. Vincent's Medical Center in New York. The experiment was carried out by Janet Quinn, Assistant Director of Nursing at the University of South Carolina. The design of this experiment tends to rule out the placebo effect. Thirty heart patients were given a 20 question psychological test to determine their level of anxiety. Then they were treated by a group trained in Therapeutic Touch. A control group of patients were also treated by sham healers who imitated the same positions as those who had training. Anxiety levels dropped 17 percent after only five minutes treatment by trained practitioners, but those who were only imitating a treatment created no effect.

Daniel Wirth of Healing Sciences International in Orinda, California conducted a tightly controlled experiment involving Therapeutic Touch. Forty-four male college students received identical minor wounds deliberately inflicted by a doctor in the right or left shoulder. Twenty-three then received a Therapeutic Touch healing and the other twenty-one did not. The treatments were given in such a way that the possibility of a placebo effect was ruled out. All forty-four students extended their arms though a hole in the wall. In the other room, a trained healer was present for those who received healing and administered healing from a distance without touching. For those who did not receive healing, no one was present in the room. Both the students and the doctor who administered the wounds and later also evaluated their healing rate had been told that the experiment was about the electrical conductivity of the body. Neither knew that the experiment was about healing. Eight and sixteen day follow-up measurements of the rate of wound healing were done. After eight days, the treated groups wounds had shrunk 93.5 percent compared with 67.3 percent for those not treated. After sixteen days, the figures were 99.3 and

90.9. After debriefing, the students stated they did not know the true nature of the experiment and had felt no contact with the healer. The possibility that expectations of the students caused the healing was ruled out.

Dr. John Zimmerman of the University of Colorado using a SQUID (Superconducting Quantum Interference Device) has discovered that magnetic fields several hundred times stronger than background noise are created around the hands of trained healers when doing healing work on patients. No such fields are created by 'sham' healers making the same movements indicating something special is happening with the trained healers. The frequencies of the magnetic fields surrounding the hands of the trained healers were of the alpha and theta wave range similar to those seen in the brain of meditators.

Dr. Barnard Grad of McGill University in Montreal, used barley seeds to test the effect of psychic healing energies on plants. The seeds were planted in pots and watered with a saline solution which is known to retard their sprouting and growth. With elaborate double-blind conditions setup, one group of seeds were watered with saline solution that had been treated by a psychic healer. The treated saline was held by the healer in a sealed container for fifteen minutes. The other seeds were watered with untreated saline. The person watering the plants did not know which group was getting the treated saline and which was getting the untreated saline. The plants watered with healer treated saline solution grew faster and were healthier producing 25% more weight and having a higher chlorophyll content. These experiments have been replicated in Dr. Grads lab and in other laboratories as well.

Dr. Grad carried out similar experiments involving tap water and plants. Sealed containers of water were given to a psychic healer to hold and others were given to a severely depressed patient to hold. The plants watered with the healer-held water had an increased growth rate and those watered with the water held by the severely depressed patient had a decrease in growth rate compared to controls.

These experiments involving plants, in addition to confirming the non-placebo nature of psychic healing, scientifically confirm the ancient metaphysical understanding that healing energies can be stored in water for future use.

In another experiment involving psychic healer Olga Worrall, Dr. Robert Miller used an electromechanical transducer to measure the microscopic growth rate of rye grass. The device used has an accuracy of one thousandth of an inch per hour. Dr. Miller setup the experiment in his laboratory and then left, locking the door behind him to eliminate any unnecessary disturbance. Olga, located over 600 miles away, was asked to pray for the test plant at exactly 9 PM that evening. When Dr. Miller returned to the laboratory the next day, the test equipment had recorded normal continuous growth of 6.25 thousandths of an inch per hour up to 9 PM. At that time, the record began to deviate upward and had risen to 52.5 thousands of an inch per hour which was an increase of 840 percent! This increased growth rate remained till morning when it decreased but never to its original level.

The Spindrift group has done extensive research involving prayer and plants. Their results indicate that prayed for plants always grow faster and are healthier than non-prayed for plants even though the conditions are equal for both groups of plants and those doing the praying are miles away. These results were consistent regardless of the distance involved and occurred over and over. They are described by Robert Owen in his book, Qualitative Research: The Early Years.

One of the interesting results of their research work is that the results were best when the prayer was non-directional, that is when the prayer was simply for the plants general well-being rather than for a specific result such as a certain growth rate or overall height.

More experiments are being done and scientific theories are being developed to describe Reiki and Reiki like healing techniques. As we continue into the new millennium, increasing interest along with more sensitive equipment will allow science to more completely understand, validate, and accept the reality of Reiki. As this happens, we will see Reiki and other laying-on hands healing techniques coming into common use by individuals for themselves and family along with its use in hospitals and doctors offices. The deeper understanding about the nature of health and the unity of all life this rediscovered age old wisdom will provide will reduce suffering and make earth a more worthwhile place to live. With this in mind, let us be encouraged to continue in the spirit of Reiki to help others and to heal the planet.

Reiki Research Papers

The following is a list of research papers on Reiki and other 'laying on hands' healing techniques.

Algarin, R., *Using REIKI as a harm reduction tool and as a stress management technique for participants and self.*, Northeast Conference: Drugs, Sex and Harm Reduction Conference Syllabus. (1995), Harm Reduction Coalition and the Drug Policy Foundation, the ACLU AIDS Project and the City University of New York.

Brewitt, B., Vittetoe, T., Hartwell , *The efficacy of Reiki hands-on healing: improvements in spleen and nervous system function as quantified by electrodermal screening.*, Alternative Therapies 1997 July; Vol.3. No.4., Available from: Hartwell Healing and Health 2850 228th S.E. #D, Issaquah, WA 98029

Bullock, M., *Reiki: a complementary therapy for life.*, Am J Hosp Palliat Care. 1997 Jan; 14(1): 31-33.

Grad, B., *A telekinetic effect on plant growth I.*, International Journal of Parapsychology *1963, 5(2), 117-134.* (The Grad studies were conducted using a talented non-Reiki healer who employed 'laying on' hands)

Grad, B., A telekinetic effect on plant growth II. Experiments Involving Treatment of Saline in Stoppered Bottles, International Journal of Parapsychology *1964(a), 6, 473-498.*

Grad, B., A telekinetic effect on plant growth III. Stimulating and inhibiting effects, Research Brief Presented to the Seventh Annual Convention of the Parapsychological Association, Oxford University, Oxford, England Sep 1964(b).

Grad, B., Some biological effects of laying-on of hands: a review of experiments with animals and plants, Journal of the American Society for Psychical Research 1965(a), 59, 95-127 (Also reproduced In: Schmeidler, Gertrude (Ed.) Parapsychology: Its Relation to Physics, Biology, Psychology and Psychiatry, Metuchen, NJ: Scarecrow 1976).

Grad, B., PK effects of fermentation of yeast, Proceedings of the Parapsychological Association *1965(b), 2, 15-16.*

Grad, B., The 'laying on hands': implications for psychotherapy, gentling and the placebo effect, Journal of the Society for Psychical Research 1967, 61(4), 286-305 (Also Reviewed In: Schmeidler, Gertrude (Ed.) Parapsychology: Its Relation to Physics, Biology, Psychology and Psychiatry, Metuchen, NJ: Scarecrow 1976).

Grad, B., Cadoret, R. J. and Paul, G. I., The Influence of an Unorthodox, Method of Treatment on Wound Healing in Mice, International Journal of Parapsyhology 1961, 3, 5-24.

Kelner, M. et al, *Health care and consumer choice: medical and alternative therapies.*, Soc Sci Med. 1997 Jul; 45(2): 203-212.

Kelner, M. et al. , *Who seeks alternative health care? A profile of the users of five modes of treatment.*, J Altern Complement Med. 1997; 3(2): 127-140.

Krieger, K, *Healing By The 'Laying-On' of Hands as a Facilitator of Bioenergetic Change: The Response of In-Vivo Human Hemoglobin*,, Psychoenergetic Systems, 1976, Vol. 1, P. 121-129, (This study uses Therapeutic Touch).

Miller, R., The positive effect of prayer on plants, Psychic 1972, 3(5),24-25.

Miller, R., Methods of detecting and measuring healing energies, In: White, John and Krippner, Stanley, Future Science, Garden City, NY: Anchor/Doubleday 1977.

Miller, R., Study of remote mental healing, Medical Hypotheses, 1982, 8, 481-490. (Also reviewed briefly in: Maddock, Peter, International Parascience Institute: Toronto and London Conferences, 1981, Parapsychology Review 1982, 13(4), 7).

Milton, G., & Chapman, E., *The benefits of Reiki treatment in drug and alcohol rehabilitation programs.*, Pathways to healing: Enhancing Life Through Complimentary Therapies, Conference Proceedings 1995 September; 24-25. Canberra: Royal College of Nursing Australia.

Neklason, Z. T., *The effects of Reiki treatment on telepathy and personality traits.*, Thesis (M.S. in Counseling) 80 pages —California State University, Hayward, 1987.

Olson, K., Hanson, J., *Reiki to manage pain: a preliminary report.*, Cancer Prevention & Control 1997; I(2) Canadian publication

Quinn, J., *One nurse's evolution as a healer*, American Journal of Nursing (Apr) 1979, 662-665.

Quinn, J., An Investigation of the Effect of Therapeutic Touch Without Physical Contact on State Anxiety of Hospitalized Cardiovascular Patients, Unpublished Ph.D. Thesis, New York University 1982.

Quinn, J., Building a body of knowledge: research on Therapeutic Touch 1974-1986, Journal of Holistic Nursing *1988, 6(1), 37-45.*

Quinn, J., Therapeutic Touch as energy exchange: Replication and extension, Nursing Science Quarterly 1989(a), 2(2), 79-87.

Quinn, J., Future directions for Therapeutic Touch research, Journal of Holistic Nursing 1989(b), 7(1), 19-25.

Rosentiel, L. , *Hypnosis and Reiki*, Journal of Hypnotism 1991 Dec.; 8-10

Schlitz, M., Braud, W., *Reiki-Plus natural healing: an ethnographic/experimental study.*, PSI Research 1985 Sept./Dec.; 4(3-4) 100-123., Available from Mind Science Foundation, 8301 Broadway, #100, San Antonio, Texas 78209

Tattam, A. , *Reiki—healing and dealing.* , Aust Nurs J. 1994 Aug; 2(2): 3.

Thorton, L., *A study of Reiki, An energy field treatment, using Rogers' Science.* 1996 Winter; Vol. VIII, No. 3., Available from: Lucia Thorton, 12592 Valley Vista Lane, Fresno, CA 93720, Email: lucia_marie_thornton@CSU.fresno.edu

Thorton, L., *A study of Reiki using Rogers' Science, Part II,* 1996 Spring; Vol. VIII, No. 4., Available from: Lucia Thorton, 12592 Valley Vista Lane, Fresno, CA 93720, Email: lucia_marie_thornton@CSU.fresno.edu

van Sell, S. L., *Reiki: an ancient touch therapy.* , RN. 1996 Feb; 59(2): 57-59.

Wetzel, W., *Reiki Healing: a physiologic perspective.*, Journal of Holistic Nursing 1989; Vol.7, No. 1 47-54., Available from Wendy Wetzel, 452 Dahlia Street, Fairfield, CA 94533

Wirth, D.P. et al. , *Wound healing and complementary therapies: a review.* J Altern Complement Med. 1996; 2(4): 493-502.

Wirth, D.P. et al., *Complementary healing therapies.* , Int J Psychosom. 1994; 41(1-4): 61-67.

Wirth, D.P., Chang, R.J., Paxton E. And J.B., *Haematological indicators of complementary healing intervention,* Complementary Therapies in Medicine 1996; 4, 14-20.

Wirth, D.P., Brenlan, D.R., Levine, R.J., Rodriguez, C.M., *The effect of complementary healing therapy on postoperative pain after surgical removal of impacted third molar teeth.*, Complementary Therapies in Medicine 1993; 1, 133-138.

* Thanks to Light and Adonea for their help in compiling this list.

Reiki in Hospitals

At hospitals and clinics across America, Reiki is beginning to gain acceptance as a meaningful and cost-effective way to improve patient care.

"Reiki sessions cause patients to heal faster with less pain," says Marilyn Vega, RN, a private-duty nurse at the Manhattan Eye, Ear and Throat Hospital in New York. "[Reiki] accelerates recovery from surgery, improves mental attitude and reduces the negative effects of medication and other medical procedures."

Vega, a Reiki Master, includes Reiki with her regular nursing procedures. Because the patients like Reiki, she has attracted a lot of attention from other patients through word of mouth, as well as from members of the hospital staff. Patients have asked her to do Reiki on them in the operating and recovery rooms. She has also been asked to do Reiki sessions on cancer patients at Memorial Sloane Kettering Hospital, including patients with bone marrow transplants. Recognizing the value of Reiki in patient care, six doctors and twenty-five nurses have taken Reiki training with her.

America's Interest in Complementary Health Care

The general public is turning with ever increasing interest to complementary health care, including Reiki. In fact, a study conducted by David M. Eisenberg, M.D. of Boston's Beth Israel Hospital found that one in every three Americans has used such care, spending over 14 billion out-of-pocket dollars on alternative health care in 1990 alone![1]

Reiki is also gaining wider acceptance in the medical establishment. Hospitals across the country are incorporating it into their roster of patient services, often with their own Reiki-trained physicians, nurses and support staff.

Why Hospitals Like Reiki

Hospitals are undergoing major changes. They are experiencing a need to reduce costs and at the same time improve patient care. Under the old medical model based on expensive medication and technology, this posed an unsolvable dilemma. Not so with Reiki and other complementary modalities. Reiki requires no technology at all and many of its practitioners offer their services for free. Reiki is therefore a very good way to improve care while cutting costs.

Julie Motz, a Reiki trained healer, has worked with Mehmet Oz, M.D., a noted cardiothoracic surgeon at Columbia Presbyterian Medical Center in New York. Motz uses Reiki and other subtle energy techniques to balance the patients' energy during operations. She has assisted Dr. Oz in the operating room during open heart surgeries and heart transplants. Motz reports that none of the eleven heart patients so treated experienced the usual postoperative depression, the bypass patients had no postoperative pain or leg weakness; and the transplant patients experienced no organ rejection.

An article in the Marin Independent Journal follows Motz's work at the Marin General Hospital in Marin County, California, just north of San Francisco. There Motz has used subtle energy healing techniques with patients in the operating room. She makes a point of communicating caring feelings and positive thoughts to the patients, and has been given grants to work with mastectomy patients in particular.

David Guillion, M.D., an oncologist at Marin General, has stated: "I feel we need to do whatever is in our power to help the patient. We provide state of the art medicine in our office, but healing is a multidimensional process . . . I endorse the idea that there is a potential healing that can take place utilizing energy."

The Tucson Medical Center's Reiki Clinic

The Reiki Clinic at the Tucson Medical Center (TMC) in Arizona has a team of Reiki practitioners who give Reiki to patients in their rooms. The program is administered by Sally Soderlund, RN, who is the Support Services Coordinator for Oncology. Arlene Siegel, who has been with the program from the beginning, runs the monthly support meetings for the Reiki volunteers.

The TMC program started in May 1995. Three Reiki Masters invited members of the Tucson Reiki community to help them start a Reiki clinic, but lacked the funds for a location. In the process of trying to solve this problem, they contacted Sandy Haywood, the hospital administrator at TMC, and offered to provide Reiki sessions for the hospital patients. Haywood had a supportive attitude toward complementary care and made it possible for the hospital Reiki program to get started.

The program first began in the Cancer Care Unit, but has since expanded to many other areas in the hospital. At first, the attending physician had to give permission for Reiki to be provided. This has changed, and now the attending nurse makes the request.

Reiki sessions are given by two-person teams as this creates a feeling of safety and confidence for both the patients and the practitioners. Patients must sign a consent form and sessions are given in their rooms while they are in bed. It is up to the Reiki team to explain Reiki to each patient before giving the treatment. They have found this usually works best by first taking a few minutes to introduce themselves and get to know the patient, then explain the work they do.

They have found it best not to use the word "Reiki" at first when describing how they can help, but to talk about healing energy. They explain how healing energy exists in the body but is depleted when a person is sick, and they describe their work as helping to increase the patient's healing energy supply. Later, after trust has been gained, they explain more about the technique and that it is called Reiki. They also play special healing music during the Reiki session.

Volunteers at the Reiki clinic have found it helpful not to use metaphysical terms when talking to patients or to hospital staff about Reiki. Terms like aura, chakras, energy bodies, etc. tend to cause confusion and mistrust. It works better to explain Reiki in everyday terms by simply saying that touching is something everyone needs and enjoys. They also found that describing their work as Reiki *treatments* tended to create some fear, whereas calling them Reiki *sessions* worked much better.

When new Reiki volunteers come in, Soderlund has them fill out a detailed questionnaire and sign a release form. Volunteers must agree not to solicit Reiki sessions from the patients for treatment outside the hospital. Then they are assigned to work with an experienced two-person Reiki team in a process they call *shadowing*. After six shadowing sessions, Soderlund goes over administrative procedures with them, giving information about how the hospital works and explaining how to interact with the hospital staff and the patients. They are also told how to deal with various issues that might arise. Then they team up with another veteran volunteer or another new volunteer like themselves to form a new two-person team. There are about twenty volunteers in the program now with two to four giving treatments at any one time.

Siegel runs monthly meetings for the Reiki volunteers. At the meetings they set goals, share experiences and go over policy such as dress code and other guidelines on conduct. They also do role playing where they develop new ways to respond to patients' questions or comments. At the meetings they have developed a questionnaire to keep track of patients' progress after receiving Reiki.

Siegel believes that each patient requires a unique response. Most of the patients are very sick, some are dying, but they all respond to their conditions differently. Conditions treated at the Reiki Clinic include cancer, pain, chronic conditions, and post-operative surgery (they also deal with childbirth).

Siegel says that "from the time we enter the patients room, the patients' best interests are uppermost in our minds. We take time to establish rapport, listen to them describe their condition and make them as comfortable as possible. Then, as we become channels for Reiki to do its work and the Reiki begins to flow, the real reason for our presence becomes apparent." She says people volunteer because of the feelings they have in their hearts and other spiritual experiences they receive by helping those in need.

The main reason the program is successful is that the patients like Reiki and request it. The patients enjoy the sessions and request more after their first experience. Some have reported spiritual experiences. Nurses also report that Reiki has positive effects on their patients including reduced pain, increased relaxation, better sleep, better patient cooperation and increased appetite. The program has been well-received by other members of the hospital staff who sense the value of Reiki and accept that it is fulfilling an important aspect of hospital care.[3]

Reiki at Portsmouth Regional Hospital

Patricia Alandydy is an RN and a Reiki Master. She is the Assistant Director of Surgical Services at Portsmouth Regional Hospital in Portsmouth, New Hampshire. With the support of her Director Jocclyn King and CEO William Schuler, she has made Reiki services available to patients within the Surgical Services Department. This is one of the largest departments in the hospital and includes the operating room, Central Supply, the Post Anesthesia Care Unit, the Ambulatory Care Unit and the Fourth Floor where patients are admitted after surgery. During telephone interviews with pre-op patients, Reiki is offered along with many other services. If patients request it, Reiki is then incorporated into their admission the morning of surgery, and an additional fifteen to twenty minute session is given prior to their transport to the operating room. Reiki has also been done in the operating room at Portsmouth Regional Hospital.

Reiki sessions are given by twenty members of the hospital staff whom Patricia has trained in Reiki. These include RN's, physical therapists, technicians and medical records and support staff. Reiki services began in April 1997 and 400 patients have received sessions to date either pre- or postoperatively.

"It has been an extremely rewarding experience," Alandydy says, "to see Reiki embraced by such a diverse group of people and spread so far and wide by word of mouth, in a positive light. Patients many times request a Reiki [session] based on the positive experience of one of their friends. It has also been very revealing to see how open-minded the older patient population is to try Reiki. In the hospital setting Reiki is presented as a technique which reduces stress and promotes relaxation, thereby enhancing the body's natural ability to heal itself."

The Reiki practitioners do not add psychic readings or other new-age techniques to the Reiki sessions, but just do straight Reiki. Because of these boundaries, and the positive results that have been demonstrated, Reiki has gained credibility with the physicians and other staff members. It is now being requested from other care areas of the hospital to treat anxiety, chronic pain, cancer and other conditions.

Alandydy, with her partner Greda Cocco, also manage a hospital-supported Reiki clinic through their business called Seacoast Complementary Care, Inc. The clinic is open two days a week and staffed by fifty trained Reiki volunteers, half of whom come from the hospital staff and the rest from the local Reiki community. They usually have thirteen to seventeen Reiki tables in use at the clinic with one or two Reiki volunteers per table. The clinic treats a wide range of conditions including HIV, pain, and side effects from chemotherapy and radiation. Some patients are referred by hospital physicians and some come by word of mouth from the local community. They are charged a nominal fee of $10.00 per session. The clinic is full each night and often has a waiting list.[4]

The California Pacific Medical Center's Reiki Program

The California Pacific Medical Center is one of the largest hospitals in northern California. Its Health and Healing Clinic, a branch of the Institute for Health and Healing, provides care for both acute and chronic illness using a wide range of complementary care including Reiki, Chinese medicine, hypnosis, biofeedback, acupuncture, homeopathy, herbal therapy, nutritional therapy and aromatherapy. The clinic has six treatment rooms and is currently staffed by two physicians, Mike Cantwell, M.D. and Amy Saltzman, M.D. Cantwell, a pediatrician specializing in infectious diseases, is also a Reiki Master with training in nutritional therapy. Saltzman specializes in internal medicine and has training in mindfulness meditation, acupuncture and nutritional therapy. Other professionals are waiting to join the staff, including several physicians.

The doctors at the clinic work with the patients and their referring physicians to determine what complementary modalities will be appropriate for the patient. A detailed questionnaire designed to provide a holistic overview of the patient's condition is used to help decide the course of treatment. The questionnaire involves a broad range of subjects including personal satisfaction with relationships including friends and family, body image, job, career, and spirituality. The clinic is very popular and currently has a waiting list of more than 100 patients.

Dr. Cantwell provides one to three hour long Reiki sessions, after which he assigns the patient to a Reiki II internist who continues to provide Reiki sessions outside the clinic. Patients who continue to respond well to the Reiki treatments are referred for Reiki training so they can do Reiki self-treatments on a continuing basis.

Dr. Cantwell states: "I have found Reiki to be useful in the treatment of acute illnesses such as musculoskeletal injury/pain, headache, acute infections, and asthma. Reiki is also useful for patients with chronic illnesses, especially those associated with chronic pain."

At this point, Reiki is not covered by insurance at the clinic, but Dr. Cantwell is conducting clinical research in the hope of convincing insurance companies that complementary care is viable and will save them money.[5]

More MD's and Nurses Practicing Reiki

Mary Lee Radka is a Reiki Master and an RN who has the job classification of Nurse-Healer because of her Reiki skills. She teaches Reiki classes to nurses and other hospital staff at the University of Michigan Hospital in Ann Arbor. She also uses Reiki with most of her patients. She has found Reiki to produce the best results in reducing pain and stress, improving circulation and eliminating nerve blocks.

Reiki Master Nancy Eos, MD, was a member of the teaching staff of the University of Michigan Medical School. As an emergency-room physician, she treated patients with Reiki along with standard medical procedures.

"I can't imagine practicing medicine without Reiki," Eos says. "With Reiki all I have to do is touch a person. Things happen that don't usually happen. Pain lessens in intensity. Rashes fade. Wheezing gives way to breathing clearly. Angry people begin to joke with me."

In her book *Reiki and Medicine*[6] she includes descriptions of using Reiki to treat trauma, heart attack, respiratory problems, CPR, child abuse, allergic reactions and other emergency-room situations. Dr. Eos now maintains a family practice at Grass Lake Medical Center and is an admitting-room physician at Foote Hospital in Jackson, Michigan, where she continues to use Reiki in conjunction with standard medical procedures. According to Dr. Eos, there are at least five other physicians at Foote hospital who have Reiki training along with many nurses.

Libby Barnett and Maggie Chambers are Reiki Masters who have treated patients and given Reiki training to staff members in over a dozen New England hospitals. They teach Reiki as complementary care and the hospital staff they have trained add Reiki to the regular medical procedures they administer to their patients. Their book *Reiki Energy Medicine*[7] describes their experiences. One of the interesting things they recommend is creating hospital "Reiki Rooms," staffed by volunteers, where patients as well as hospital staff can come to receive Reiki treatments. Bettina Peyton, MD, one of the physicians Libby and Maggie have trained states: "Reiki's utter simplicity, coupled with its potentially powerful effects, compels us to acknowledge the concept of a universal healing energy."

Anyone interested in bringing Reiki into hospitals is encouraged to do so. The hospital setting where there are so many people in real need is a wonderful place to offer Reiki. The experiences and recommendations in this article should provide a good starting point for developing Reiki programs in your area.

Endnotes

[1] *Eisenberg, David, et al. "Unconventional Medicine in the United States."* New England Journal of Medicine 328, no. 4 (1993), 246-52.

[2] *Ashley, Beth. "Healing hands,"* Marin Independent Journal, May 11, 1997.

[3] If you have additional questions about the Reiki Clinic at TMC, call Sally Soderlund at (520) 324-2900.

[4] If you have questions for Patricia, you can contact her at 1-603-433-5175. There may be a slight delay in response because of her busy schedule, but she will get back to you.

[5] Mike Cantwell, M.D. can be reached at 1-415-923-3503.

[6] Unfortunately, her book is no longer in print.

[7] *Barnett, Libby and Maggie Chambers with Susan Davidson,* Reiki Energy Medicine, Healing Arts Press, Rochester, Vermont, 1996. Libby and Maggie are at the Reiki Healing Connection, 1-603-654-2787.

Was Jesus a Reiki Master?

I tell you the truth, anyone who has faith in me, can do the same miracles I have done, and even greater things than these will you do. John 14-12

One of the outstanding aspects of Jesus' life was the miracles he worked. According to the Bible, Jesus walked on water, fed five thousand people with five loaves of bread and two fishes, changed water to wine and raised people from the dead. However, the most meaningful of his miracles were the healings he performed. These healings include: paralysis, lameness, fever, catalepsy, hemorrhage, skin disease, mental disorders, spirit possession, deafness and blindness. Many of these healings were accomplished by the laying on hands. This is indicated frequently in the New Testament. Luke 4:40 states: "When the Sun was setting, the people brought to Jesus all who had various kinds of sickness, and laying his hand on each one, he healed them."

In Matthew 8:14-15, Jesus uses touch to heal Peter's mother-in-law of a fever. In Mark 1:40-42 Jesus uses his hands to heal a man with leprosy. This is also mentioned in Luke 5:12-13. Matthew 20:29-34 describes how Jesus healed two blind men by touching their eyes and in Mark 8:22-25 Jesus uses his hands to heal another blind man. In Mark 7:32 35 he uses touch to heal a man who is deaf and can't speak. In Luke 7:12-15, Jesus raises a dead man by touching his coffin and in Luke 8:49-55 Jesus uses touch to return a dead girl to life.

There are many similarities between the laying on hands healing Jesus did and the practice of Reiki. One important similarity is the fact that Jesus could pass the power to heal on to others. We read in Luke 9:1-2 that Jesus gave his twelve disciples power to drive out all demons and to cure diseases. We do not know by what process Jesus gave healing power to his disciples, but the fact that he was able to pass it on to them indicates an important similarity with Reiki.

Another aspect of Jesus' healing practice that is similar to Reiki relates to faith. While faith was required for many of the healings he performed, it appears that the healings Jesus did with his hands did not require faith. Mark 6:5-6 states: "He could not do any miracles there, except lay his hands on a few sick people and heal them. And he was amazed at their lack of faith." So, in spite of the fact that they did not believe, Jesus was still able to use laying on hands to heal. This is one of the important aspects of Reiki: It does not require faith on the part of those receiving a treatment in order for the Reiki to work.

The fact that Jesus had secret teachings he gave only to those who he had given healing power is clearly indicated in Matthew 13:10-11 and Mark 4:10-12 & 34. Secret knowledge is also part of the Reiki teachings in that the symbols as well as the process of doing attunements are secret.

It is not known whether Jesus was born with the ability to heal through touch or if this was something he acquired. His activities between age twelve and thirty are not mentioned in the Bible. It has been suggested by several researchers that during this time Jesus traveled to the East and was schooled in many of the mystical teachings of India, Tibet and China. If this is so, it is possible that Jesus was initiated into Reiki, or a Reiki like practice during this time as Reiki evolved out of practices originating in India, Tibet and China.

The early followers of Jesus' teachings were made up of several groups. One such group was the Gnostics. They practiced laying on hands and professed to have a secret knowledge that had been passed on to them by Jesus and his disciples. The Gnostics were made up of many smaller groups some of which were known as the Docetists, the Marcionites, and the Carpocratians. They were united by their core beliefs which included: a personal experience of Jesus or the "kingdom of heaven within," their freedom and lack of rules, guidelines or creeds and their reliance on inspiration and inner guidance. Their existence is attested to by the Gnostic gospels which are part of the Dead Sea Scrolls as well as a letter written in the second century AD by the early church father, Clement of Alexandria. In Clement's letter, he spoke of a secret gospel of Mark which was based on the normal canonical one but with additions for special followers of Jesus, referred to as "those who were being perfected" and "those who are being initiated into the great mysteries."

When Christianity became organized after the second century, its teachings were centered around faith and the official teachings of the church, rather than healing or "good works" and inner guidance as practiced by the Gnostics. At this time, those promoting the organization of the church began subduing and killing those Gnostics who would not conform with the authority of the newly developing church. With the elimination of the Gnostics and the establishment of the Christian church, the practice of laying on hands by Christians was lost.

Jesus possessed great confidence in his ability and was able to heal in an instantaneous way with spectacular results. It is clear that he had perfected many metaphysical skills and used them in conjunction to get the results he created. Was one of those skills Reiki? Was Jesus a Reiki Master in addition to being a spiritual Master? While it cannot be established in an absolute sense that Jesus was a Reiki Master, the available evidence clearly indicates so many similarities that it is likely the laying on hands healing Jesus practiced must have been very closely associated with an early form of Reiki. The teachings of Jesus, as well as the example he set are a great inspiration for us. As we continue to perfect our spiritual awareness and allow our inner wisdom to guide us, it is likely that breakthroughs will occur, eventually bringing with them the quality of healing that Jesus had.

Since the above article was written, additional information has come from author George Katchmer who has done some very interesting research. According to George, after Jesus passed his healing abilities on to his disciples, these abilities were later incorporated into the Persian Nestorian Church of the East where they continued to be practiced. The Church of the East sent out missionaries who specialized in medicine and healing. From the 7th to the 13th centuries AD, they sent their missionaries throughout Asia including China, Tibet and Japan. Their teachings and healing practices were very popular and became incorporated into the religious practices of those countries. In Tibet, the Church of the East established a Bishop of Tibet and George Katchmer has found many references to Christianity throughout Asia and the fact that these Christian teachings were mixed with Buddhism. From this information it is easy to see the possibility that the healing techniques of Jesus were eventually incorporated into Tibetan Buddhism and then found their way to Japan and Dr. Usui. This adds some very interesting information: The possibility that Reiki may have come from a combination of Buddhist and early Christian teachings. George is writing a book about this which gives a more detailed description and includes all his sources. His book should be out in 1999.

Reiki as a Spiritual Path

In life, we often encounter crossroads where difficult decisions must be made. A new direction needs to be taken. Uncomfortable choices have to be considered.

We may find ourselves in a job we don't like, a relationship that no longer feels supportive of our best interests, or other situations that undermine our health, energy or self-confidence. We wonder how we got there. At the same time we aren't sure what to do and feel there are no positive alternatives.

One of the most important, yet least explained, benefits of Reiki is its ability to guide your life in a way that is exactly right for you. When you focus Reiki on difficult situations in your life, guidance about what to do comes more easily. Or it may inspire a change in attitude or belief about your situation. Suddenly, you see your condition from a fresh perspective, one which reveals a previously unseen course of action leading to a more positive result. For many practitioners, the flow of Reiki has helped them develop and strengthen parts of their character, enabling them to deal with difficult challenges in a more positive way. Reiki not only provides the necessary information, but also the right kind of personal energy to take the needed action.

Our lives are created from the effects of all the decisions and actions we have taken, not only in this life, but in past lives as well. Every action has an effect which eventually comes back to us. If we adopt the philosophy and accept the fact that ultimately, we are responsible for everything we experience in life, we will be centered in our power and be better able to create positive and lasting change in our lives.

Negative experiences are actually our own actions coming full circle. Use the wisdom and love of Reiki and you will be able to more easily take responsibility for them. Reiki will guide you to heal and balance the energy in a way that is healthy for you and everyone involved. This prevents the fostering of additional negative actions on your part and breaks the vicious downward spiral that only leads to deeper levels of the disempowered victim state. These seemingly negative experiences contain important lessons for us— in fact, they are exactly the lessons we need to learn in order to progress on our spiritual path! There are no accidents.

Shortly after learning Reiki I moved to California and began an NLP practice. Things went well for a while, but after a year or so I found myself with no money. I called my parents and asked them if they could loan me the money I needed to keep my practice going. A week later they had an answer. They could not loan me any money, but I could come back to Detroit and live with them. They thought it was a great solution as they had been wanting me to come home for a long time. To me it was the worst thing I could imagine. I had moved away from Detroit to get away from them. Having to move from California to Detroit to live with my parents was an overwhelming thought. I was forty years old. I had no money. I had lots of negative feelings about my parents and in fact felt they were the cause of most of my problems. I did not think I could do it.

However, I began sending Reiki to the situation and began meditating about it. The Reiki energy allowed me to think more clearly and I was directed to think about the responsibility I had for my situation in life and for my own growth. I knew that many of our issues have come from our parents. The father usually affects ones issues with career, money, responsibility, discipline, etc. and the mother affects ones issues with relationships, nurturing, intuition and creativity among other things. I also knew that if one could restimulate ones issues, thus bringing them up to the surface, they could more easily be dealt with and healed.

I came to the conclusion that although it would be very difficult, moving back with my parents would also be a great opportunity for deep healing to take place. With the help of Reiki, I decided to accept my parents invitation and move in with them. I also decided I would maintain a positive, optimistic attitude and be actively looking for opportunities to heal so I could learn the lessons life was presenting to me as quickly as possible.

Many difficult situations did come up, but with the help of Reiki, I was able to turn them into healing and learning experiences. I lived with my parents for nine months and was able to heal several major issues. After moving out, but staying in the area, I continued to work on our relationship and over a period of years, things became much more loving and understanding between us. This has greatly contributed to my happiness in other areas of life as well.

Many fortunate experiences took place because of my move back to Detroit. The spiritual community in Detroit was larger than what I had imagined and I met many people with similar interests who were supportive. Reiki directed me to begin sharing my experiences in metaphysics with others. I began writing articles for the local metaphysical paper and teaching classes in spiritual development. Eventually I met a Reiki Master who was charging a very reasonable fee for Reiki Master training. I took her training and began teaching Reiki classes. This lead to the development of the Center and the expansion of my career. Reiki helped me step by step to change a personal crisis into a fulfilling purposeful life.

Opportunities to connect with our spiritual path are continually coming to us through our every day experiences. All we need to do is recognize them. Allow Reiki to guide you and its gentle energy will help you learn the lesson and release you from the need to revisit the negative experiences again. At the same time, you will move forward on your spiritual path. However, if you project blame for your problems on others, and choose to act like a victim, your misinterpretations will block the flow of energy and make it virtually impossible to get good guidance. When one is in *victim consciousness* it is very difficult to create positive outcomes.

There is a plan for your life that is exactly right for you and supports your continual improvement. This plan has always existed and when you are ready to discover and follow it, the universe meets you where you are and adjusts to your needs at the moment. Reiki will always lead you in the direction of your unique life plan, which is actually your true spiritual path, based on your unique requirements as an individual.

The purpose of your spiritual path is to connect you to your true nature which is the love, wisdom and power that is within you. Identification with a deeply healed self is the goal of your journey.

In order to achieve this, it is necessary to heal or release all the parts of yourself which are not deeply healed. Reiki can guide you through this process, supplying the needed understanding and the healing.

Reiki is able to surround your life and everything you do with a wonderful glowing radiant energy that smooths the way, making things easier than you thought it could be. At times, spontaneous events bring solutions that contain all the factors necessary for resolution and success. This is a wonderful multidimensional process that can effortlessly produce those seemingly lucky breaks where you just happen to be in the right place at the right time and say the right things to receive positive results.

Not only can Reiki guide your life, it fosters opportunities to receive greater benefit from the abundance around you. Reiki leads you to do things you thought you would never do, things you believed were too difficult yet are necessary if you are to grow as a person. As Reiki nurtures your greater personal growth, you become capable of achieving more and your life becomes a continuous process of increasing enjoyment and satisfaction.

There are many ways to use Reiki on your spiritual path. The most basic is to do Reiki self treatments every day and ask for guidance. Include a prayer such as "Guide me and heal me so that I might be of greater service to others." Continue to think of Reiki through-out the day. Visualize it flowing within and around you. As you do this, add the distant symbol and direct Reiki to the important events or people in your life asking that they be blessed. You can also direct the flow to your life in general. This will act to heal the issues that are current for you and prepare you for those that will be coming up. The soothing energy of Reiki will help you feel more relaxed and place you in a more resourceful state where you will be better able to deal with issues as they come up and take advantage of opportunities as they arise.

Reiki soothes relationships as well. As you practice Reiki, those you deal with will be delighted to discover you have become a more enjoyable person to be with and your relationships will begin going more smoothly. The effectiveness of all other healing or self improvement programs you are involved with will improve. With Reiki energy flowing continually in your life, steady improvement of your health and well being as well as every aspect of your life can be expected over the long term. Amazing things happen when you practice Reiki everyday.

Another action that will help you on your spiritual path is to create good Karma by helping others. One way to do this is to meditate in the morning on the distant symbol with the intention that Reiki will flow through you all day long to all those who need it. Whenever you have a spare moment during the day, reinforce this process with the same meditation. Just visualize or draw out the distant symbol and affirm over and over, "I continually send Reiki energy to all those who need it." You will be pleasantly surprised to find your Reiki affecting those around you as well as going to people you have never met. A happy satisfying feeling will come as you realize that others are benefiting from your commitment to Reiki.

Another beneficial process is to use the distant symbol to send Reiki to enlightened beings such as Jesus, Mother Mary, Buddha, Krishna, or God. Once you feel the energy flowing, ask them to help you fully express their enlightened nature in your everyday life. Or you can ask your own enlightened self to help you assume its enlightened nature as your true identity.

Reiki energy comes directly from the highest spiritual source. It works in harmony with all other spiritual techniques by increasing their effectiveness. It can guide you on your spiritual path. By carefully considering the decisions and actions you take and allowing Reiki energy to guide you, a life filled with joy, beauty and peace is yours to create.

May your life be guided by the greatest wisdom and love.

So be it.

Reiki for Peace

We live in a world where peace seems to be in short supply. Looking around us we find there is no lack of conflict and turmoil resulting in many difficult problems. There are problems with health, relationships, family, work, crime etc. Problems seem to exist in every area of life leaving people feeling unhappy, unfulfilled and dissatisfied, thus making it difficult to get along with others and to cope with life. This lack of peace also exists in our social and political systems causing war and struggle between nations and groups all over the planet. As we look at the history of the world, we see that this seems to have always been the case from the beginning of civilization. People feeling unhappy, unfulfilled and unsatisfied with life, struggling with each other and never finding lasting peace even though they actively seek it.

People want to be happy, they want to be at peace and from inside ourselves there comes a feeling that there must be a way. So people keep trying, and sometimes temporary solutions are found, but lasting, meaningful peace so often escapes us. Like trying to catch a rainbow in a jar or hold the ocean in our hands, our efforts seem to lack a basic understanding.

The reason peace is so hard to find is that the underlying assumption about what will bring peace is false. This false assumption is that peace will come by establishing and defending our separateness; separateness from other individuals, other ethnic groups, other religions, other countries, etc. This causes unnecessary fear and unhealthy competitiveness towards others. We feel we must either fear others or dominate and control them to prevent them from penetrating the false barrier we have created to preserve our separateness. This concept is so pervasive in our society that it has become an unconscious compulsion that most don't even know they are acting on.

Thus, it has been felt that peace will come only when "our" group dominates all others. This has been true between nations as well as between ethnic groups and even religions. In fact, major problems have been caused by one religion trying to dominate all others-thus starting wars and causing great human suffering in the name of peace.

The assumption of separateness is an assumption without a soul. It creates the illusion of a world filled with separate pieces with no common essence to connect the pieces with each other so they can work in harmony. Therefore, peace is not possible as long as this assumption is acted on.

The truth is we are not separate, we are all interconnected and interdependent. Native peoples have known this all along. We are part of a web of life. Any change in one part of the web affects all other parts. Modern science has discovered this too. In the science of Chaos theory it's been discovered it is possible for a butterfly in China to flap its wings and in a few days create a hurricane off the coast of Florida. We are all connected. The connecting link between all living things are the forces of nature and most importantly, the life force. All people and all living things have the life force, the God force flowing through them. This is why we should respect all people, all groups, all life. We have life flowing through us and we are all connected and dependent on each other. This is the truth, peace will never come on earth by one group, nation or religion dominating all others. Peace will only come when we have respect for all other groups, nations and religions.

The way to create peace on an individual level as well as between groups and nations is to accept that we are not separate and peace will not come from defending our separateness, but from acknowledging our interdependence, our oneness. Our ability to create peace will come only from taking action on this understanding. Every group, religion and nation has value and should be honored and respected for their unique expression. Every group is precious.

Since life force is the connecting link between all people and all living things and Reiki is life force guided by God, Reiki can have a powerful healing effect for peace. Because Reiki comes from the unlimited source of life, Reiki is powerful enough to heal any conflict and to restore peace to any situation. Reiki respects and honors all living things. Reiki can heal and repair the life connection between all individuals, groups and nations. Reiki can be sent at a distance to any individual, group or world problem to create peace. Therefore, I encourage all Reiki practitioners to work together in harmony to create world peace. Our web site contains a "Global Healing Page" where we ask all Reiki practitioners to send distant Reiki to global conflicts and crisis situations. The use of Reiki reconnects people to the universal source and to each other. We can make a difference. Please use your Reiki to create peace.

I am working with a jewelry artist to create a special Reiki grid. This piece is being made to send healing to all people on earth and to create world peace. It will be made of copper, silver and gold. It is shaped like the heart chakra with 12 petals, and will have 12 crystals pointing outward with a 12 sided pyramid in the middle. There will be 12 symbols, one behind each crystal to represent the major religions of the world including Buddhism, Hinduism, Christianity, Judaism, Taoism, Shintoism, Islam, Zoroastrianism, the goddess religions, independent spiritual paths, native peoples and one for all others including agnostics, atheists, and unknowns. It will be charged with Reiki.

In early May, 1998, I will be taking it to the North Pole. While there, I will be further charging it with Reiki, meditating with it and praying. I will pray to God and to all the founders of all the worlds religions asking that all the followers of all religions and spiritual paths work together to create peace among all people on earth. After it is charged and prayed for, I will take a photograph of it, thus capturing its essence so that others will be able to use copies of the photo to continue charging it with Reiki and to pray for world peace. The picture will be available on our web site and free copies will be available to anyone who asks. Eventually, the ice will shift and break up and the World Peace Crystal Grid will sink to the bottom of the Arctic Ocean in the vicinity of the North Pole. There it will remain forever sending Reiki to create and maintain world peace.

World Peace Crystal Grid Placed at the North Pole

A cold wind whipped across the gravel runway as I walked from the plane to the small airport terminal at Resolute in Canada's Northwest Territory. It had taken two days to get here after teaching a Karuna Reiki® class in New York City, yet I still had over eight hours of flight time left before I would get to my destination - the North Pole, where I planned to place a specially created crystal grid dedicated to world peace. The terminal was filled with activity. A women's relay team, which was cross country skiing to the Pole, was exchanging team members - one team arriving and one leaving. As I spoke to our organizer, I noticed that although I did not feel weak and my mind was clear, my vision and hearing were phasing in and out going from normal to almost black then back to normal. I realized that my system was attempting to adjust to the unusually high vibration of the area. At this latitude and time of year, the sun is always up and simply circles around a little above the horizon 24 hours a day. This combined with clear skies most of the time, blazing white snow and it's proximity to the North Pole, created an environment filled with intensity.

The temperature ranged from ten degrees above to ten degrees below zero F. which is not that cold, but with the wind chill, it can get much colder. The remainder of the journey would be in a "Twin Otter," a very rugged and powerful plane known as the "workhorse of the Arctic. " It is equipped with retractable skis so it can land on both gravel runways (which is all they can have up here because of the permafrost) and snow or ice. Because good weather is important in order to land on the ice at the Pole, our departure time could change at a moment's notice. My ride up to the North Pole was possible because of an extra seat on the plane that would pick up a dog sled and cross country ski team that was going there. Although we were scheduled to leave the next afternoon, a sudden change in weather put us on the plane in the early morning. We left and stopped at the Eureka weather station on Ellesmere Island to refuel, then had to stay overnight as the weather changed again. We continued on the next day and landing on the Arctic ice, picked up the dog sled team - loading the dog sled, and dogs onto the plane along with the team members and proceeded on. The team had not made it to the Pole, so we were going to fly the remainder of the distance and land there. However, when we got over the Pole, it was covered with fog and the pilot could not see the ice clearly enough to land, so we circled and came back.

Not having placed the "Grid" at the Pole, I was disappointed and not sure what to do. So I made a call to the Center asking people to send Reiki energy to help the project, then I talked to the flight dispatcher to see if I could get on another flight.

There are actually two North Poles, one is geographic and one is magnetic. I chose the geographic pole simply because this was the

pole I was offered a ride to, but then we were unable to land. I did not know there were flights to the magnetic pole even though I knew this would be the best place for the "Grid." After Reiki had been sent, the situation changed. The flight dispatcher, being sympathetic to our cause, convinced the people going to pick up a Frenchman who was walking to the magnetic North Pole to allow me to go along on the flight. The magnetic North Pole is near Ellef Ringnes Island.

After landing, I walked out away from the plane on sea ice. There I dedicated the World Peace Crystal Grid and gave it a final charging of Reiki. A picture was taken as it lay on the snow at the magnetic North Pole, copies of which are now available. A video tape was also made. Then it was buried under the snow. When the sea ice melts in July, it will sink to the bottom of the ocean where it will remain forever. The dedication was as follows; "I dedicate this World Peace Grid to create peace among all people on earth. May all people realize that they come from the same source and because of this, may the members of all nations and all nationalities and the members of all religions and all spiritual paths and the members of all groups value and respect each other and work together to create peace among all people on earth. May the founders of all religions and spiritual paths work together to create peace among all people on earth. May the followers of all religions and spiritual paths work together to create peace among all people on earth. May all those who view this World Peace Grid be deeply healed and may they be empowered to create peace among all people on earth. I now place this World Peace Grid at the North Pole to remain forever creating and maintaining peace among all people on earth.

The World Peace Crystal Grid is made of solid copper in the shape of the heart chakra, 12 inches in diameter and plated with 24 carat gold. A 12 sided quartz pyramid is at the center under which are inscribed the Usui power symbol and the Karuna peace symbol. Double terminated quartz crystals are on each petal. Inscribed around the center are symbols for all the world's religions and the words: "May the followers of all religions and spiritual paths work together to create peace among all people on earth."

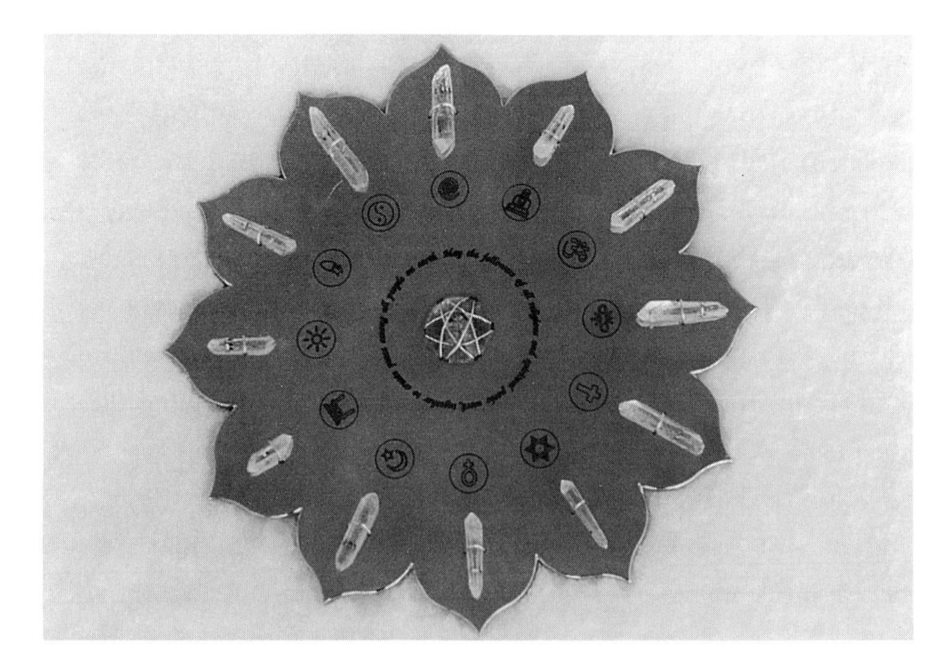

The World Peace Crystal Grid is in a tremendously powerful location. All the magnetic energy of the earth flows through this area and continues to circulate all around the earth. This is perhaps the strongest power spot in the world! When you send healing energy to the Grid through the picture, your healing energies are sent out to circulate around the planet in a greatly amplified way. Because the purpose of the Grid is to create peace among all people on earth, and you are one of those people, it will also send healing directly back to you.

The Earth's Magnetic Field

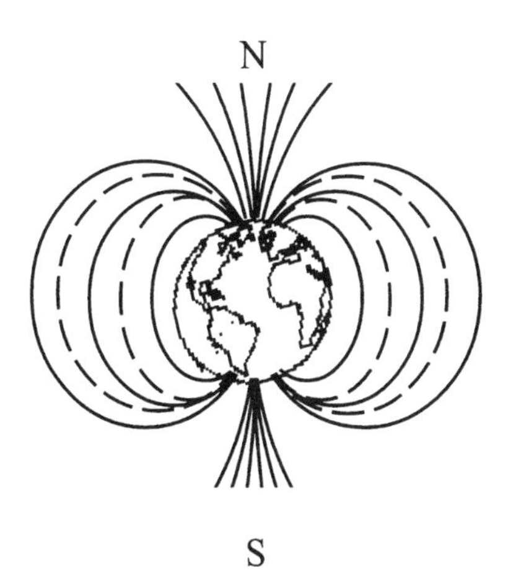

After receiving a copy of the glossy photo, try sending Reiki to it using the Usui distant symbol or try pointing a crystal at the central crystal in the picture and send healing in this way. Also, meditating on the picture or having it in your healing room will have a valuable healing effect on you or those in the room. Place it under your Reiki table or carry it with you and charge it whenever you have some free time. Also try giving the World Peace Grid a Reiki attunement. As more people send healing to the World Peace Crystal Grid, more healing will be going out to maintain peace in the world. As you meditate with the Grid, you may be guided in new ways to use the Grid - try them.

If you would like a free color photo of the Grid, taken at the magnetic North Pole, just let us know. Additional copies are $1.00 each, 8" x 10" are $10.00, and 20" x 30" are $50.00.

When the World Peace Crystal Grid was made for the North Pole, one was also planned for the South Pole and two 12 sided crystals were cut from the same tabular crystal for use at the center of each grid. Because the central crystals are cut from the same piece of quartz, the grids for both Poles will be naturally attuned to each other. Plans for the South Pole are forming, but it is likely not to take place for another year or so.

If we are to create peace on earth, it will be important for us to take the time to really understand and appreciate all groups of people. This includes other nationalities, other religious and spiritual groups and groups of every kind. If you are a Reiki practitioner, remember it is important that there be harmony between all Reiki people regardless of organization or lineage. The Grid can be used for this purpose as well. The better all Reiki practitioners and Masters work together in harmony to heal each other and the planet, the more successful we will be.

We are at a critical time in the history of the earth. If the human population is to survive and also to prosper, we need to truly value and respect each other. Every person and every group of people on earth has something of value to contribute and until we realize this and really respect all groups of people, we will not be able to be at peace within ourselves or to create peace in the world. As harmony grows between some groups, it will be easier for others until the process is complete. Once there is peace among all people on earth, a tremendous time of prosperity and well being will ensue not only for people, but for all living things.

Religious and spiritual symbols on the World Peace Crystal Grid

Native Peoples

Shintoism

Judaism

Hinduism

Zoroastrianism

Islam

Christianity

Buddhism

Taoism

Goddess Religions

Independent Spiritual Paths

Unknowns and all others

The Changing Way of Reiki

Serenity often comes from a sense of knowing that we are honoring the gifts we have been blessed with. When we feel inner stirrings to do more, to expand our abilities, so we can make the contribution we were brought to this life to make, we must then choose. Do we ignore this guidance, in the name of tradition, or do we change and grow?

The search for serenity has brought many to study and practice Reiki. However, the more we work with Reiki, the more we are guided to let it develop our skill, out of this development comes the changing way of Reiki.

Reiki is a Japanese system of natural healing based on channeling healing energy through the hands. Reiki healing energy is a special kind of healing energy that has its own consciousness and does not need to be guided by the practitioner. Reiki simply guides itself by communicating with the clients higher self and using the information received to adjust itself for the specific needs of the client. Because of this, the practitioner does not have to decide what to do or how to do it, and simply allows the Reiki energy to flow through, trusting in its innate wisdom. Furthermore, one does not learn to channel Reiki energy in the same way other things are learned. The ability to channel Reiki is simply passed on to the Reiki student through the Reiki Master during an attunement process. After that, the student is shown how to place the hands and how to allow the intelligence of Reiki to guide the practitioner in giving a treatment. This truly marvelous system of healing is so simple that virtually anyone can learn to do it.

The practice of Reiki has gone through a process of evolution since it was brought to the western world by Mrs. Takata in 1938. After World War II, Mrs. Takata was the only practicing Reiki Master in the western world. Therefore, anyone who wished to study Reiki in the West had just one teacher to study with. When she began training other Reiki Masters in 1970, she charged $10,000 for the Reiki Master training. Due to problems surrounding the war with Japan and the conditions of her Reiki training, she chose to teach in a very rigid way, discouraging her students from experimenting and strictly requiring them to practice exactly as she taught them. She explained that if they varied from the technique in anyway, they would not be doing Reiki. Innovation and the development of new techniques was discouraged.

Mrs. Takata was a very adept Reiki Master who had a lot to offer her students. However, taking notes or the use of tape recorders was not allowed in Mrs. Takata's classes. She also taught her Master to teach the same way she taught and to require students to study with just one Reiki Master. Her Master, not having any written material or notes to work from, and not wanting to make mistakes, tended to pass on a little less information than what they were given. As this process continued from teacher to student, Reiki began to lose vitality.

The rigidity, allegiance to one Master and the high fees tended to keep the emphasis of Reiki more on a hierarchy whose purpose was to rigidly preserve a tradition rather than to openly develop one's ability to heal and help others.

The beginning of Reiki in the western world may seem restrictive in some ways, but the important thing is that it did get started. We are grateful to Mrs. Takata and the Reiki Masters she trained for the sacrifices they made and their dedication to teaching Reiki. This style of Reiki continues to be taught by a few and is appropriate for some people and provides an important aspect to the overall expression of this healing art.

Although its beginnings were somewhat stifling to the spirit of Reiki, the *Reiki energy began to heal its own expression.* As more people were trained and began using Reiki, the nature of the energy itself began to influence how it was practiced. Reiki energy, being very flexible and creative, treating each unique situation with a unique response and working freely with all other forms of healing, inspired those same qualities in its students and teachers. Many, trusting in their inner promptings, began to break away from the rigid way they had been taught and tried new things. Some teachers began training with more than one teacher and exchanging information among themselves. Lower, more reasonable fees were instituted. Others began experimenting and adding to their practice, knowledge and healing skills they had learned from other systems of healing or had acquired from inner guidance. By developing new Reiki techniques, depth was added to their understanding and they developed their own style thus improving the effectiveness of their healing abilities.

Through innovative, intuitive development, deeper levels of Reiki guidance were uncovered bringing to the surface the understanding that Reiki can guide your whole life, creating beauty, abundance and health on every level. When these teachers taught, they passed on their new information and skills to their students. Because they had the courage to follow their inner guidance, vitality has been added to the system of Reiki, which is allowing it to remain healthy, to grow and develop. In this way, the practice of Reiki is evolving as the Reiki energies heal and guide those who practice it.

The process of evolution that the system of Reiki healing has followed is similar to the system of martial arts training of the Japanese Samurai. According to the "Heiho Okugi Sho," a manual used by the Takeda Samurai, at the first or lowest level of training called Heino-Tsukai, the Samurai studies with just one teacher and practices only what is given to him. He also passes on to his students only what he was taught, adding nothing of his own experience. At this level of training, it was found that the system gradually declined over time due to a lack of vitality.

The highest level of training was called Heiho Sha. At this level, the Samurai studies deeply from many teachers, and experiments on his own to develop his technique to even greater levels of effectiveness. When he trains others, he passes on what he has learned including his personal additions. At this level, the system is filled with vitality and continues to develop over time. Because Reiki comes from Japan, perhaps the same spirit that guided the Samurai in the development of their system is now guiding the development of Reiki.

While the healing energy used by Reiki practitioners remains the same, it should be kept in mind that the experience and range of healing skills each has developed can be quite different. A few practitioners have remained with the style of Reiki taught by Mrs. Takata while others are of the more recent school where study with many teachers is emphasized and the development of personal style is present.

When choosing a Reiki healer or teacher, it is important to find out if they are part of a true Reiki lineage, leading back to Dr. Usui. Even more important is the extent of their training, how long they have been practicing, how much they charge, and exactly what you will receive from them.

Ask to talk to some of their clients and students to find out what they received and if they are happy with it. The most important thing to depend on when choosing a practitioner or teacher is your own inner guidance. Do you feel comfortable with the person's energy, and do they have a true desire to help you?

As reality continues to unfold, created by the combined intention of the world mind reflecting on its own nature, it is fascinating to observe the many varieties of spiritual practice that are becoming available to the aspiring student. Let us be ever mindful of the increased freedom the changing nature of our choices brings to us and call on inner wisdom to guide us to ever deeper levels of joy and peace.

The Original Reiki Ideals

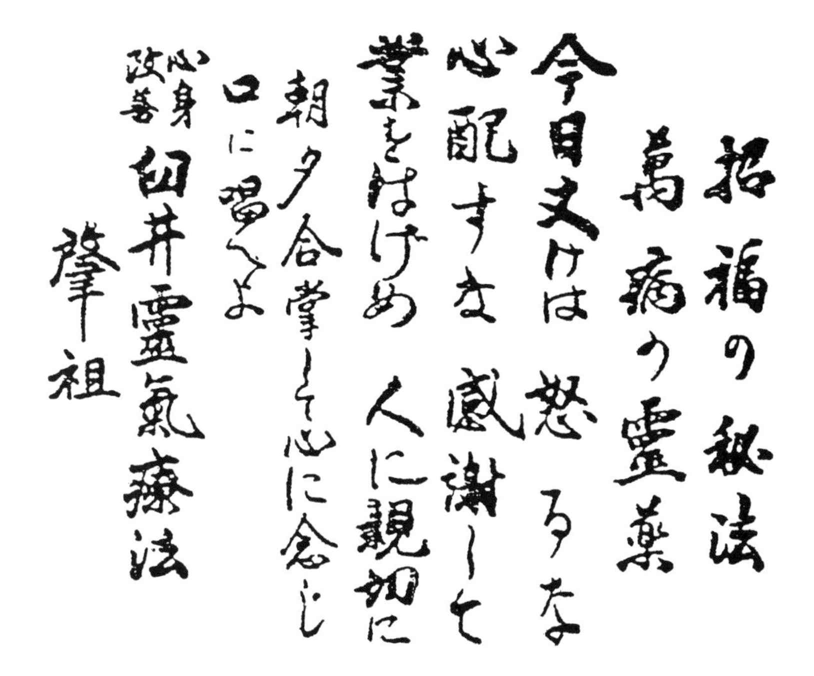

The secret art of inviting happiness

The miraculous medicine of all diseases

Just for today, do not anger

Do not worry and be filled with gratitude

Devote yourself to your work. Be kind to people.

Every morning and evening, join your hands in prayer.

Pray these words to your heart

and chant these words with your mouth

Usui Reiki Treatment for the improvement of body and mind

The founder , Usui Mikao

These are the Reiki Ideals used by Reiki Masters in Japan. It was provided by a Japanese Reiki Master, Toshitaka Mochizuki in conjunction with his Reiki book, "Iyashi No Te" (Healing Hands). On the previous page is a line for line translation of the Reiki Ideals starting from the right

Mochizuki has researched the history of Reiki and has come up with some interesting information that differs from the history of Usui Reiki as told by Mrs. Takata and also adds to it. Part of his information comes from another book "The Secret of How to Take Care of Your Family Members" by Takichi Tsukida although I am told that the current edition is mysteriously missing the information about Dr. Usui. Both books are in Japanese.

According to Mochizuki, Dr. Usui was born August 15th, 1865 in the Gifu district. He died at age 62 on March 9th, 1926 in Fukuyama, Hiroshima. Dr. Usui was not a Christian. He was most likely a spiritualist and psychic. People who do his kind of work were called "Rei Jyutu Ka" which means, "people who have spiritual skill." It was during his activities as a spiritualist that he rediscovered Reiki on Kurama-yama, a sacred mountain outside Kyoto. He established a healing society in Tokyo in 1922 and started giving treatments. Usui created the three degrees or ranks of Reiki which he called Shoden (First Teaching), Okuden (Inner Teaching), and Shinpiden (Mystery Teaching). He moved to Nakano, Tokyo in 1925 and expanded his healing center.

Dr. Usui was well known for his healing abilities and was often invited to local cities to speak and do healing work. Dr. Hayashi was given the attunements for all three Reiki degrees by Dr. Usui in 1925 when Dr. Hayashi was 47 and just one year before Dr. Usui passed on.

There were many 'Hands on Healing' schools in Japan before the war. These other schools were not part of Usui Reiki. "Taireido" was started by Tanaka Monihei, "Tenohira-Ryouchi-Kenkyuka" which means "The Association for The Study of Palm Treatments" was started by Eguchi Toshihiro who learned healing from Dr. Usui and then founded his own group. Toshihiro also wrote some books on healing which are now hard to find. "Jintai-Ragium-Gakkai" which means "The Human Body Radium Society" was founded by Matumoto Chiwake and "Shinnoukyou-Honin" was the name of a religious group founded by Nishimura Taikan. His method was called "ShinnouKyou-Syokusyu-Shikou Ryoho" which means "Violet Light Healing Method."

Mochizuki teaches a form of Reiki from the Takata lineage and has studied with several western Reiki Masters including one of my students. However, he does not teach the same as I do. The Reiki being taught in Japan is mostly a combination of various western Takata Reiki styles with some Japanese Reiki added.

He indicates that there are still those from non-Takata lineages who are practicing in Japan including those from the Hayashi lineage and also from the Usui lineage. Members of these groups are very secretive and do not easily or quickly pass on what they know. The important thing about any form of Reiki is not where it came from, but how effective is it as a healing system. Also of importance is how openly the information is presented and if those who teach it act in a Reiki like way.

Mochizuki indicates that he got the original Reiki Ideals from a non-Takata Reiki group he associates with, but did not indicate where they got it from. However, there is an indication from another source that the original Reiki Ideals are written on linen and now hang in a private shrine. Also, we have a handwritten copy of the Usui Ideals that is said to be written by Dr. Usui's own hand. I am certain that within the next six months or year our search for the "True History of Usui Reiki" will be even more fruitful and we will be finding out much more about Dr. Usui and how he originally practiced.

Discovering the Roots of Reiki

As teachers and practitioners of Reiki Laura Ellen Gifford and myself have enjoyed sharing the "traditional" story of the history of Reiki as taught in the West. However, this story has never felt complete to us and this feeling has been expressed by many others as well. Important information seemed to be missing and parts of the story didn't seem to fit. Some of the "facts" have been investigated, and found to be untrue and much has been unverified.

The information about Dr. Usui, or Usui Sensei as he is called by Reiki students in Japan, has been so limited and myth-like in the West that some people have wondered if he ever really existed. This has made it difficult to feel connected to him and the roots of the system he created.

Last year we published an article on the "Original Reiki Ideals" which revealed a more authentic version of what we had been given in the West. Since then additional information has been uncovered. Some of this new information is from the investigations of Dave King, Melissa Riggall, Robert Jefford, and others. The most interesting and verifiable of this new information is from Frank Arjava Petter and his new book, "Reiki Fire." Arjava was one of the first western Reiki Masters to teach other Master in Japan starting in 1993.

With the help of his Japanese wife, Chetna and Shizuko Akimoto, a Japanese Reiki Master, Arjava contacted a number of important sources of information concerning the history of Reiki. Included were several people who learned Reiki from some of Usui Sensei's early teachers, namely a Mr. Tsutomo Oishi and a Mr. Fumio

Ogawa. Arjava also spoke to members of Usui Sensei's family and members of the Usui Shiki Reiki Ryoho, which is the original Reiki organization started by Usui Sensei in Tokyo. From these contacts he filled in some missing information on the history of Reiki and discovered other valuable facts. This information provides more accurate insight into who Usui Sensei was, what motivated him to rediscover Reiki and how he and his students practiced.

After reading Arjava's book, we were interested in knowing more and e-mailed him with many questions. He answered our questions and invited us to Japan to visit the sacred sites and discuss the implications of this new information. We gladly accepted and flew to Japan the second week of September, 1997.

Many synchronistic events occurred in connection with our trip to Japan starting with someone faxing us important pages from Arjava's book. After our trip was scheduled, we met people who lived in Japan who offered to act as additional guides. One such person, Yuki Yamamoto, flew from Osaka, Japan to the Center to attend a Karuna Reiki® class, but knew nothing about our planned trip. Osaka is close to Mt. Kurama and Yuki had been there many times. When he found out about our planned trip, he offered to join us at Mt. Kurama with his car and be our guide.

Just two weeks after meeting on the Internet, Friedemann, who lives in Japan came to the University of Kentucky on business, and visited Laura at her Healing Center in Kentucky to exchange Reiki sessions. At this time we had not planned our trip to Japan. It turned out that Friedemann lives only 10 minutes from where Arjava lives in Japan and also offered to help us at Mt. Kurama!

So, without seeking it, we had several extra guides that proved to be very helpful! We feel these things happened as a result of our daily Reiki practice during which we invite the energy to guide every aspect of our lives.

Mt. Kurama - Where Reiki was Rediscovered

According to literature at the Mt. Kurama temple, in 770 A.D. a priest named Gantei climbed Mt. Kurama, led by a white horse. His soul was enlightened with the realization of Bishamon-ten, the protector of the northern quarter of the Buddhist heaven and the spirit of the sun. Gantei founded the Buddhist temple on Mt. Kurama which went through many stages of development and restoration and now contains many temples and pagodas. The temple was formerly part of the Tendai sect of Buddhism. Since 1949, it has been part of the newly founded Kurama-Kokyo sect of Buddhism.

Arjava, Yuki and Friedemann accompanied us to Mt. Kurama during our several trips to the mountain. Mt. Kurama has wonderful energy! The Kurama temples are located up the side of the mountain requiring that one hike up and down the mountain to visit the temples. This would normally be very tiring, but we found that taking a moment to rest quickly restores one's energy. Mt. Kurama is truly a "power spot" and the energy that flows is very uplifting yet calming. There is a feeling of contentment and peace. We both were aware of many helpful spirits from whom we received inspiration and guidance.

Our first stop up the mountain was at the San-mon Station. There is a shrine there representing the Trinity which, in the Kurama-

Kokyo Buddhist sect, is known as Sonten or Supreme Deity. Sonten is thought to be the source of all creation - the essence of all that is. Sonten came to earth in the form of a being over six million years ago when Mao-son, the great king of the conquerors of evil, descended upon Mt. Kurama from Venus. His mission was the salvation and evolution of mankind and all living things on earth.

Mao-son is also said to have incarnated as the spirit of the earth, residing inside an ancient cedar tree at the top of the mountain. This spirit emanates from Mount Kurama to this day. Sonten manifests on earth as Love, Light and Power. The love symbol is called Senju-Kannon and looks very similar to the Usui Mental/ Emotional symbol. The light symbol is called Bishamon-ten and is represented by a Sanskrit symbol we were not familiar with. The power symbol is called Mao-son and is represented by an older version of the Om symbol. The essence of all three is in each one. These three symbols are similar in meaning to the three symbols of Reiki II.

The kanji for the Usui Master symbol is also used in the Kurama temple literature. The meaning of Sonten is expressed using the same kanji we use for the Usui Master symbol. During a temple prayer in the Hondon temple, we were given special permission to be present as the priest used the name of the Usui Master symbol during part of his chant!

It has to be more than a coincidence that the Usui Master symbol is used by the Kurama temple to represent Sonten, the Supreme Deity and that the symbol which represents love looks very similar to the Usui mental/emotional symbol. Since Usui Sensei received his Reiki initiation on Mt. Kurama, it is likely he made use of some of the symbolism and philosophy of the Kurama temple in the formulation of Reiki.

In fact, the understanding we received from Shizuko Akimoto is that Usui Sensei studied many things before rediscovering Reiki. He took what he studied and combined what seemed right into the Usui system of healing. This is apparent in the "Reiki Ideals" which we now know came from the Meiji Emperor. This is indicated in the inscription on the Usui memorial, located at Saihoji temple. This inscription also indicates Usui Sensei studied many things, but his life was not going well when he decided to go to Mt. Kurama to meditate for answers. Perhaps he was looking for a personal transformation for which the mountain is noted and for help in healing his life. It seems he did what many of us have done when our lives have not gone well and looked to the spiritual for answers and healing. He opened himself to the higher power and not only received a healing for himself, but a way to help others.

Mt. Kurama is covered with giant cedar trees. As we hiked upward, we passed through a section of the trail near the top of the mountain covered with roots and we thought, yes, the roots of Reiki. At the top of the mountain there is a quiet place with a small shrine called Okunoin Mao-den where Mao-son is said to have descended. Behind the shrine protected by an iron fence is an old cedar tree said to contain the spirit of Mao-son. This area is very calm and has the sound of running water and wind blowing through the trees. We spent a long time here meditating and giving Reiki treatments and attunements to each other.

The Memorial - Answers Carved in Stone

With the help of Arjava Petter, we found the memorial dedicated to Usui Sensei, the founder of the Reiki healing system. It is located at the Saihoji Temple in the Suginami district of Tokyo. The memorial was created by the Usui Shiki Reiki Ryoho shortly after Usui Sensei's transition. This is the organization which Usui Sensei started to promote the practice and teaching of Reiki. The memorial site is maintained by the Usui Shiki Reiki Ryoho. This was verified by officials of the Saihoji Temple where the memorial is located. We were surprised that the Usui Shiki Reiki Ryoho still exists because part of the "traditional" story stated that all the members of this group died in the war or had stopped using Reiki and that Mrs. Takata was the only remaining teacher of the Usui system in the world. We now know the Usui Shiki Reiki Ryoho has always existed and still exists today. They have been teaching and practicing Reiki in Japan all this time.

The memorial consists of a large monolith about four feet wide and ten feet tall. On it, written in old style Japanese kanji, is a description of Usui Sensei's life and his discovery and use of Reiki. It is located in a public cemetery at the Saihoji Temple next to Usui Sensei's grave stone where his ashes, along with those of his wife and son, have been placed. The inscription on the memorial stone was written by Mr. Okata who is believed to be a member of the Usui Shiki Reiki Ryoho and Mr. Ushida, who became president after Usui Sensei died. There are many important and interesting details included in the inscription.

We went to the memorial site with flowers and burned sage. A butterfly came and landed on the flowers we brought and it felt very peaceful as we drew all the Usui Reiki symbols and sent Reiki to Usui Sensei. We held hands and prayed for Reiki and Usui Sensei to guide us in writing this article and sharing a more accurate understanding of Reiki worldwide. We asked for this new information to help unite all Reiki practitioners in harmony and to inspire them to use Reiki to heal each other, all people of the world, and the earth as a whole. While meditating, we became aware of Usui Sensei with a bright light all around him. We felt he was very happy that an image of his memorial would be seen by so many and that a clearer understanding of how he practiced Reiki would be known.

Shizuko Akimoto shared additional information about Usui Sensei and the history of Reiki. According to her research with Mr. Ogawa and other members of the Usui Shiki Reiki Ryoho, there was never a mandatory fee for Reiki treatments. Dr. Hayashi charged whatever people could pay and if they were poor, he treated them for free. His Reiki business was not lucrative, but was done out of a desire to help people. Many of his students received their Reiki training in return for working at his clinic. If Usui Sensei became popular helping people who suffered from the Tokyo earthquake as it states on his memorial, it is likely that he did not insist on everyone paying a fee for his treatments, but like Dr. Hayashi, must have treated many for free.

There is no title of "Grandmaster" or "Lineage Bearer" in the organization started by Usui Sensei.

The high fees for Master level charged by some in the West are not a requirement of the Usui Shiki Reiki Ryoho. Also, Usui Sensei and Dr. Hayashi are known to have had class manuals that were given to students, but which have not yet become available to us.

Since Reiki was not a lucrative business, some of Dr. Hayashi's students were forced to stop practicing Reiki due to a lack of adequate income. This suggests that a middle financial path may be more appropriate. A middle path allows one to charge reasonable fees so that one can earn a living, yet be able to lower fees when appropriate or to charge nothing for those unable to pay. This allows people to dedicate their life to doing Reiki full time, thus creating more adept healers who are able to help more people.

According to Arjava Petter, there is no title of "Grandmaster" or "Lineage Bearer" in the organization started by Usui Sensei. The person in charge of the organization is the president. Usui Sensei was the first president of the Usui Shiki Reiki Ryoho. Since then, there have been six successive presidents: Mr. Ushida, Mr. Taketomi, Mr. Watanabe, Mr. Wanami, Ms. Kimiko Koyama and the current president is Mr. Kondo who accepted the office in 1998. Dr. Hayashi was a respected teacher, but was not a president and had no other responsibilities.

Language and cultural differences along with a reluctance on the part of the Usui Shiki Reiki Ryoho to speak with western Reiki practitioners has restricted our communication. This is why information about the original Usui Reiki organization has taken so long to surface in the West. However, some communication has occurred and a breakthrough is expected soon as the inscription on the Usui memorial states it is Usui Sensei's wish that Reiki be spread throughout the world.

This new information about Reiki confirms what many of us have intuitively known all along - the main focus of Reiki is to help others, and because of this there is no need to always require payment for treatments or training if the person is in need and unable to pay. Mandatory high fees for the teaching level are not a requirement. Reiki was not always an oral tradition and both Usui Sensei and Dr. Hayashi had written material they gave to their students. Attunements and the practice of Reiki are based more on intuitive guidance and intention than on rigid rules with the Reiki energy being the defining element. The flexibility of the Usui system makes it broad enough to include a wide range of methods and techniques, thus validating the many different styles being practiced today. The leadership for Reiki lies in Japan where it originated, not in the West.

The Usui memorial, the information it contains and the energy of Mt. Kurama provide us with an enduring legacy that unites us with Usui Sensei and the spirit of Reiki he rediscovered. This connects us to the roots of the Usui system and provides grounding, which keeps Reiki organic and connects us to the living energies of its origin. The Usui memorial with its inscription provides a focal point for all Reiki groups to look to as a common link, helping to heal the fragmentation and competitiveness which has developed in the West.

Indications of other important discoveries have also made themselves known. We have received reports that the written material of Usui Sensei, Dr. Hayashi, and others has been discovered and will soon be translated and shared. More open communication is likely to occur with members of the Usui Shiki Reiki Ryoho including the president which is bound to reveal additional useful information.

This is the most wonderful time for Reiki in the West now that we are finally learning the real story of Reiki. Many are feeling a wonderful sense of coming home. May we all share in the joy of these new discoveries and allow them to inspire and empower our Reiki practice.

Reiki, A New Direction

Because of significant changes taking place in the Reiki community - and the public in general - I believe Reiki is on the verge of the acceptance many of us have dreamed of, yet never thought possible. Reiki, over the next several years, could become so universally accepted that whenever a challenge comes up, most people will immediately think to use Reiki to solve it. As the acceptance of Reiki continues to evolve, I believe it will become a commonly accepted practice in medical care, education, business, law enforcement, government, the military – even world politics! This, of course, would signify a dramatically transformed world. I know many of you think this is a little far fetched, but let me explain.

New Historical Facts Strengthen Reiki

Achieving harmony within the Reiki community is one of the most difficult challenges we have had to address over the years. A lack of harmony between groups is believed to have originated when various Reiki organizations enforced restrictive rules and promoted the concept of a Reiki Grandmaster, who was thought to be in charge of Reiki. These manipulations were used in an attempt to make followers of one group believe that only they had the true Usui system of Reiki and that all other groups were invalid. Unfortunately, these strategies were counterproductive creating fear, distrust and unnecessary competitiveness between many Reiki groups. This thinking produced a poor professional image, created confusion - and in short - weakened the Reiki community as a whole. Clearly, this kind of behavior went against the very spirit of Reiki.

One of the key factors causing lack of harmony amongst groups was the lack of an accurate and verifiable history. Without solid facts, all we had to go on was the westernized perception of Reiki history – and that was so inadequate it did not even provide a firm connection to Reiki's origins in Japan. This version raised many doubts about the history of Reiki and caused some to question if Dr. Usui had even existed.

However, the discovery of Dr. Usui's grave, and especially his memorial stone, has given us verifiable information about him, how he discovered Reiki and how he practiced it. These discoveries have helped to heal the distrust among the various factions of the community, and have strengthened our universal understanding of Reiki.

Additional information about the history and practice of the Usui System of Reiki has been provided by several Japanese Reiki Masters, whose non-western lineage goes back directly to Dr. Usui. These Masters have indicated that many of the restrictive concepts, promoted in the West as part of the original Usui system - including the idea of a Reiki Grandmaster - appear to have been added after Reiki was brought to the West and are therefore, not a valid part of the original system.

Obtaining these historical facts has created a tremendous freeing effect on most Reiki practitioners (we must respect those who chose to ignore the restrictive rules; their actions are now validated by these historical discoveries) and firmly establishes that no western group or person is in charge of Reiki. It also confirms that all Reiki groups have value. Most followers have found these discoveries to be a wonderful revelation. Some practitioners from different lineages and organizations who previously would not talk to each other due to wrongly perceived differences, are now communicating freely, exchanging ideas and support. Where once there was confusion and conflict, now there is wonderful growing feelings of freedom, empowerment and community.

This newly proven heritage is also leading to a greater confidence being felt about Reiki in general. Many practitioners are becoming inspired to invest more time and energy into the development of their Reiki practices. True feelings of joy are welling up in Reiki people all over the world as they realize that because of this new supportive spirit within the Reiki community, their desire to help others can now be more easily accomplished. The Reiki community is becoming reoriented into a stronger, more vital force that is able to share Reiki with the rest of the world.

Masters' Fees

The value being provided by recent discoveries concerning the history of Reiki, is adding to a process that has been developing over a longer period of time. When Reiki first began being taught in the West, it was common for a $10,000 fee to be charged for the Master level training. The high fee was thought to be a necessary part of the Usui system (one of the ideas that has proven to be false). However, in the mid-80s Iris Ishikura, one of the Masters initiated by Mrs. Takata went against this rule and began charging a much more reasonable fee — in some cases, she even taught the Master level free of charge. The result was the Masters she taught,

taught others, also at a very reasonable fee allowing Reiki to spread very quickly. At times it appeared to be growing almost exponentially. Reiki has now spread all over the planet and is practiced by well over one million people – and the numbers keep growing.

General Public Accepts Reiki

Until recently, growth in the practice of Reiki has come mainly from members of the New Age/Metaphysical Community who already had a core belief system that could easily allow them to understand and accept Reiki. Over the years, there has been a shift in the belief system of the general public, allowing for greater acceptance of alternative medicine. As a result, we are seeing a growing interest in Reiki from the public at large. People from all backgrounds are coming for treatments and taking classes.

I can remember when I first started practicing Reiki in the early 80's. Whenever I began describing the practice of Reiki, I found people would appear noticeably distressed. I often got the impression the uninitiated thought I was a charlatan and what I was practicing was sacrilegious. Today, however, I not only find a genuine interest in Reiki, but almost everyone has at least some awareness of it. Now, when I tell people about what I do, they almost always have a positive response, or add that they know someone who practices it. More and more frequently, I am meeting people who have taken Reiki classes.

This trend was brought into focus by a research report done by Dr. David M. Eisenburg of Boston's Beth Israel Hospital. His study found that in 1990, 80 million people in the United States had used one or more forms of complementary health care, including Reiki. This group had spent more than $14 billion out-of-pocket for this care. This shift in public acceptance appears to be increasing as more and more people are becoming aware of the value of Reiki and other forms of complementary care.

Doctors, nurses and other licensed health care professionals are taking notice as their patients are asking questions about alternative forms of healing and many professionals are accepting its value. In fact a growing number of doctors and nurses have taken Reiki training and routinely include Reiki along with standard medical procedures.

Because of the public's acceptance, the news media are now taking a positive attitude toward Reiki and have featured spots on Reiki. This is a far cry from the past when, if Reiki was mentioned at all by the media, it was presented as a weird practice done by people on the fringe. I have recently seen a number of television spots on Reiki and have personally received a growing number of requests for interviews.

Scientific Validation

A perception that Reiki is not scientific, but is instead based on superstition and quackery, has caused many to question its validity.

When they are made aware of the positive results Reiki has provided, the scientific community often dismisses these results as only the placebo effect. These unfair perceptions about spiritual healing are dispelled in a new book, *Spiritual Healing, Does It Work, Research Says Yes,* by Daniel Benor, M.D.

In his book, Dr. Benor describes more than 200 scientific experiments in the field of Spiritual Healing, many of which show positive results. Many were conducted as double blind experiments which rule out the placebo effect and others were done on plants which are known not to be affected by placebo. Some of these experiments have been replicated. See page 158 for more information about this valuable new book.

I believe that once the scientific validation of spiritual healing is widely disseminated, Reiki will become more respected and the demand for Reiki training will rise dramatically. It will more easily find its way into use by every area of society. There will be opportunities to develop Reiki programs, specifically designed for education, business, law enforcement, government, the military and world politics.

This validation and acceptance will open the door to more scientific research, which in turn will produce many new discoveries. Reiki displays many qualities that science cannot explain. Because of this, research into Reiki is bound to lead to new theories about the nature of reality. This will revolutionize how mainstream society thinks. And this in turn will create new attitudes, values and beliefs in every area of human activity.

In effect, the wide spread acceptance and use of Reiki, which is beginning to take place now, will greatly quicken the manifestation of the paradigm shift that we have been waiting for. Reiki will create peace on earth and provide benefits we haven't even thought of. It will help usher in the greatest era the world has every known!

Popularity Creates Challenges

These significant changes are also creating challenges for the way Reiki is practiced. The fact that many Reiki Masters have disregarded the restrictive rules of the past and are teaching and practicing Reiki according to their own inner guidance, has generally had a positive effect on the practice of Reiki.

However, some Reiki Masters have begun teaching with reduced standards and few ethical principals. They teach classes of an hour or less in duration, with little offered except the attunement. We have received reports that all levels of Reiki including I, II and Master are being taught in one weekend or even in a day by some Masters. This leaves the students of those classes with little understanding of what Reiki is, or how to practice it. These students go on to attempt to practice Reiki without all the necessary information or training, simply abandon Reiki or even worse, pass the debased training they received onto others.

While some motivated, yet ill-informed students who realize that important information was missing from their class do seek out reputable teachers to receive additional training, this should not have to happen. There have been other reports of Reiki Masters misrepresenting what the student will receive in class, unfair competitive practice between Reiki Masters, the use of Reiki as a foil for sexual and child abuse and other ethical problems. As Reiki becomes more popular, and the general public begins to become interested, it is important that these challenges be resolved before they worsen. If these problems are not solved, the general public may develop a negative attitude toward Reiki. The positive potential Reiki offers to solve humanities problems and help create the wonderful world described above, could be greatly reduced or even lost.

A National Reiki Organization

One solution to these challenges is the creation of a national Reiki organization. Due to the breakthroughs concerning the verified history of Reiki and its harmonizing effect on the Reiki community mentioned above, conditions are now present for such an organization to work.

We are moving from a third chakra based society to a heart chakra based society; from a society based on power to a society based on love. If a Reiki organization such as this is to succeed into the future, it must be based on love and express the true spirit of Reiki.

I believe that for this organization to be successful, it would need the following: It must be open to all Reiki people regardless of lineage or organization affiliation. A board of directors could be set up from a cross-section of all Reiki groups and independents. Membership could be available for individuals and organizations.

Also, if smaller organizations develop, as is likely, then a coalition of the smaller groups would be beneficial. They could pool their resources and work together in harmony for the common good of all Reiki people.

To solve the challenges mentioned above, it would need to have a minimum set of training and teaching standards and a code-of-ethics. The teaching and training standards could indicate the minimum subjects necessary to be taught in a class and the minimum number of hours required. It would be important to keep these standards simple and reasonable, but they would be necessary if membership were to have value. The ethical standards would include things like honesty in advertising, honoring all Reiki people and groups, not requiring the client to disrobe, not touching the genital area, etc. Individuals who joined would agree to abide by these standards and code-of-ethics. Organizations who joined or who formed a coalition would agree to maintain these standards for their members.

Such an organization, or coalition of organizations, could also monitor legislation that might affect Reiki and take action to keep Reiki free of unnecessary governmental interference. It could also guide any developments in the field to keep the spirit of Reiki a part of the practice.

I have been networking with a small group of people who have expressed interest in establishing such an organization and also with existing organizations who would like to form a coalition and I will keep you posted about what develops.

The Greatest Healing the World has Ever Known

As the population of the earth increases and the uses of technology continues to improve and grow, powerful changes are happening so quickly throughout the world that it often becomes mind boggling trying to understand it all. It is important for us to step back and evaluate all the implications.

Distance is no longer a barrier. We are traveling more, and our developing communication technologies including satellite TV, Internet sites and email allow ever greater numbers of users access to all the diversity of people and ideas the world has to offer. More individuals have greater access to information and they are exchanging it with larger groups of people around the world. This is stimulating creativity and openness worldwide and having a profound effect on people's attitudes, values and beliefs. As more understanding and knowledge is shared, many people are becoming dissatisfied with their current state and are seeking change. Others are gaining power to decide their own fate and to create the kind of life they prefer.

Good Things are Happening

The break up of the Soviet Union is one example of the effect that modern communication systems are having upon the world. Satellite television broadcasts by CNN, permitted under Glasnost, allowed the Soviet people to discover how affluent westerners were in comparison to them. This fostered greater discontent with their government, and the people demanded change.

The unexpected by-product of instantaneous, global communications has been a safer world. Prior to the collapse of the Soviet Union, the USSR and the United States had thousands of nuclear warheads aimed at each other. Other sites around the world were targeted as well. A misjudgment, a short temper or a computer glitch could have reaped total worldwide destruction in a matter of hours. Many of us grew up with this nightmare in the back of our minds. The fear of nuclear annihilation undermined our plans and skewed our trust in the future. With the threat of nuclear holocaust greatly reduced, large numbers of people are convinced that their efforts to make the world a better place will have lasting value.

The world has changed in other ways. In the recent past, the major superpowers of the world either started wars with each other or helped smaller countries to initiate and wage wars. Now only the smaller countries instigate war, with the major countries playing the role of peacemakers.

These effects seem to be influencing a greater momentum toward peace in the world. After decades of violence, the recent peace settlement in Northern Ireland is a sign that this is taking place. Also encouraging is the fact that Israel and Palestine have not given up on their peace process.

The end of the cold war and the resurgent feeling of more safety and trust in the world are thought to be at least partially responsible for the steady growth of the stock market. Economic development, safer water and sanitation and improved health services have caused stunning improvements in the health of people worldwide. The World Health Organization reports that average global life expectancy has gone up from 48 years in 1955 to 66 years currently and should continue to climb to 73 years by 2025. This, of course, brings new sets of problems. However, it also generates its own solutions. As people live longer, they will be more concerned about long range solutions for our environmental problems rather than short term fixes. We can expect better care of the planet and a healthier environment as a result.

Interest in Spirituality Increasing

As technology continues to develop and increase in use, human needs are still going unfulfilled. We are becoming aware that technology cannot solve every problem. People are realizing that the most important solutions lie within! To maintain balance in a highly technological world, people are seeking out ways to express and nurture more of their own inner, personal selves. Interest in spiritual things, including Reiki and other forms of energy work, is increasing worldwide. It appears that we are moving toward a world where our drive for technological development will be balanced by our need for spiritual wholeness.

"Our drive for technological development will be balanced by our need for spiritual wholeness."

Improvements in communication also bring the possibility for quickened spiritual growth. In the past, a person was lucky to even hear about a spiritual teacher. Now the motivated seeker can easily learn about and meet any number of spiritual teachers and choose from a large number of possible paths and schools. This greater range of choice allows the aspiring devotee to find a spiritual path that is more in harmony with their life style and temperament. The mutual support and synergistic effect many schools of spiritual development have on each other creates a stimulating environment and an enriched experience for anyone involved in personal development.

Earth Changes Not Likely

It is becoming less likely that global earthquakes, polar axis shifts and the dramatic changing of oceans and continents will produce catastrophic earth changes. The time for many of these prophesied world disasters has already passed. Edgar Cayce who had a remarkable ability for clairvoyantly diagnosing illness and prescribing cures made several predictions for world disaster. Until recently, his prophesies were the main scenarios for proponents of cataclysmic earth changes. Cayce predicted that Atlantis would rise in 1966 or 67. This never happened. Even 30 years later, there is still no sign that the lost continent of Atlantis is emerging and the Cayce Foundation has taken a stance that the earth changes scenario is not likely to take place as anticipated.

Destructive earth changes were predicted by Nostradamus as well. While many of his predictions have come true, they seem to have stopped taking place since just before the Harmonic Convergence in 1987. For example, he predicted worldwide drought and famine in "...the year of the [Halley's] comet." People would be so hungry they would eat each other. Millions would die worldwide. It would be one of the most horrible disasters the earth has ever known. Halley's comet appeared in 1986. There was drought and famine in Ethiopia that year, but no global disaster. Nostradamus also foresaw a horrible earthquake and volcanic eruption with widespread death and destruction in California in May of 1988. This never happened either. Even the Jehovah's Witnesses have changed their policy concerning the end times. After previously predicting the end of the world several times, they are no longer expecting the final judgment any time soon.

We create our own reality. This is true on an individual level as well as on a global level. The primary mechanism that causes this to happen is our state of consciousness; how healthy our attitudes, values and beliefs are about ourselves and the world around us.

The danger of destructive earth changes has passed. This has happened, I believe, because of the widespread use of Reiki and all the other healing energies and prayers that have been sent to the world. The grace of God has come into play to affect positive change and reduce suffering. The result has been a healing of the global consciousness to the extent that the physical destruction of the earth is no longer a possibility. The destructive earth changes prophesies would have taken place had the global mind set remained the same as when the prophesies were given.

Look for future earth change prophecies to be more positive, relating to a massive and positive change in the way the world is organized and in our concepts about the world and ourselves!

A Transformed World

When we review the events that have taken place this century, especially in the last decade, it is clear that the fear, competition, greed, separateness, ego and power which largely motivated our world is being transformed by love, cooperation, compassion, wholeness, trust and helpfulness. This expansion of consciousness is indicated by the improvements in the health and longevity of the people of the world, the increasing interest in the spiritual side of life and the other major changes toward peace indicated above. As these positive changes continue to occur and accelerate, the quality of global consciousness will continue to rise. Many people think we are rapidly moving toward a phase transition in consciousness. They believe that the increasing communication between people worldwide is creating an ever expanding field of global awareness, and a point will be reached where world consciousness will suddenly shift to a completely new state. Examples of the phase transition effect are present in many things. When water rises in temperature, it remains liquid until it reaches 212 degrees F. Then a sudden change occurs. Water transforms into a more expanded and mobile state. It becomes steam.

The same may be happening to the global state of consciousness. As the current trend continues and people move toward a greater expression of spiritual values, we could suddenly experience a phase transition in consciousness where the whole population of the planet becomes enlightened all at once! I believe this is coming and the time will soon arrive when all countries and religions will value and respect each other. Many religions and spiritual paths point to an event like this in the near future.

"A glorious life on earth with the deepest levels of happiness will be constantly experienced."

This will be a world where the underlying motivation of all people is love, and peace is constantly present. The understanding that all things on earth are connected and affect each other will be wisely considered before decisions are made. The well-being of all people will be the most important goal. The global population will stabilize at a sustainable level with everyone healthy and leading productive, satisfying lives. A glorious life on earth with the deepest levels of happiness will be constantly experienced.

Change Causes Suffering

Major changes, even positive ones can bring about difficulties, confusion and suffering. As people, organizations, religions, and political systems adjust to new conditions, they are required to think and do things they have never done before. Sometimes the new ways go directly against cherished beliefs or religious convictions. When old structures disappear, or go through radical adjustment, unexpected crises take place. For many, this makes change very difficult. The stress and suffering that takes place when one is adjusting to a new positive state is called a "healing crisis." This applies to individuals as well as to the planet as a whole. Most of the suffering in the world today is really part of a healing crisis. For example, ethnic tensions have always been present in Bosnia, but they were prevented expression by the Soviet Union. When it dissolved, the ethnic groups were free to vent their anger and hate toward each other with horrible suffering for all. Their suffering is a great lesson for everyone. On the positive side, the major countries of the world acted to halt the bloodshed in Bosnia rather than taking sides and promoting violence as they have done in the past.

Improvements in the world economy also made the Asian monetary crisis possible. It too, has caused suffering and confusion. Yet, when it happened, countries around the world formulated a bailout plan and made billions of dollars available to solve the problem. The world is acting on the concept that mutual cooperation between countries is an important element in the success of our global economy. We are moving toward a world where in order for any one country to experience health and well-being, all countries must experience health and well-being.

Another example of improved technology and its availability producing a crisis is the nuclear testing in India and the aggressive response from Pakistan. This brings up the specter of nuclear nightmares of the past. Hopefully, those new countries who develop nuclear weapons will have the wisdom not to use them. Otherwise, a new danger - the possibility of limited nuclear war fought by third world counties - looms ahead. The tension around this issue is likely to affect how people think and the decisions they make.

Other dangers exist in our changing world. The threat of terrorists using biological, chemical or nuclear weapons, the outbreak of global epidemic's, even the possibility of comets or asteroids striking the earth are likely to develop, as well as other dangers not yet foreseen.

The inner connectedness of all things is one of the important lessons being learned now. We are becoming conscious that our inner thoughts as well as our outer actions have an affect upon others worldwide. The healthier each group of people is, the better it is for all.

Reiki can Help the Process

As the number of Reiki people increase in a room, the strength of each person's Reiki also increases. In a similar way, as the number of Reiki practitioners grow throughout the planet, the healing energy coming from each person will greatly increase. At least one million Reiki practitioners are presently in the world. There is no question that this has helped bring about much of the new peace and cooperation. In the next five years, the number of Reiki practitioners could easily increase to over ten million. The potential for Reiki to heal the world is becoming greater all the time!

Reiki can be sent at a distance. This allows all of us to send Reiki to world crisis situations as soon as we hear about them. As more people do this, suffering is reduced. Note: The global healing section on our website has a list of world crisis situations. You can help by sending Reiki to them. Also, the World Peace Crystal Grid placed at the magnetic North Pole can by used to send healing energy to the earth.

Reiki is an ideal tool to ease suffering as the world goes through its healing crises. Reiki's miracle working power transforms the fear of change into trust and love. Reiki greatly reduces discomfort and helps people open their hearts to compassionate actions. Reiki comes from the spiritual world where unity in all things is a reality. It also understands the aspects of any problem or difficulty and knows all the resources and solutions which are available. Because of this, Reiki can easily guide the world into harmony and productive cooperation. When we are confused and afraid, Reiki guides us into positive solutions. It's amazing! Reiki works in conjunction with all other forms of healing, guidance and help. Its gentle power is loving and kind. It actually possesses all the qualities the world needs for the coming New Age of peace and prosperity. Qualities of love, compassion, wisdom, justice, cooperation, humility, persistence, kindness, courage, strength and abundance are contained in Reiki energy and inspires and develops these qualities in those it treats.

The world is transforming. A New Age of peace is coming. By sending Reiki to speed the process, we quicken the pace of change and reduce suffering. As we direct our loving Reiki energy toward helping the world transform, we quicken our own transformation as well. Reiki is simple and easy to use. Let us keep upper most in our minds the tremendous good Reiki can have locally and globally. Be willing to send Reiki whenever you feel guided. By doing this, know that you are helping create the greatest healing the world has ever known.

May we all be united in love as we proceed into the new millennium.

The International Center for Reiki Training

In 1988 I founded the Center for Spiritual Development. In 1991 the name was changed to the Center for Reiki Training as Reiki became our only focus. In 1997, because of all the classes being taught abroad, "International" was added to our name.

The Reiki training offered by the Center is based on the original Usui system of Reiki. However, the Center has also added innovations that have been proven to increase Reiki's effectiveness as a healing art. These include scanning, beaming, meditation, a technique called aura clearing that removes negative psychic energy, healing attunements and acknowledgment of the role played by spiritual beings in the healing process. Brief descriptions of scanning, beaming, aura clearing and healing attunements are included below.

The attunement process used by the Center in all Reiki Level I, II, ART and Master classes is a combination of the Usui system and a special Tibetan technique. In the Reiki III/Master class, the Usui/Tibetan method of giving attunements is taught along with the original Usui system of attunements. Students wishing to practice the original Usui system of Reiki can easily do so as all additions to the Usui system are clearly explained in class.

Additions the Center has made to the original Usui system came because of inner guidance and our desire to provide greater value. They were added only after they had been thoroughly tested and were proven to enhance healing. The following techniques are ones I developed at the Center.

Scanning and Beaming

Scanning is a way of finding those places in yourself or others which are most in need of healing, then administering Reiki to them. Beaming is a way to focus Reiki energy either on the aura or on specific areas of the body.

Aura Clearing

The presence of negative psychic energy in the body or the aura is the cause of most illness and dysfunction. We therefore developed aura clearing, a Reiki technique for removing negative psychic energy. Formerly called Reiki psychic surgery, this highly effective process uses Reiki energy to empower the hands so that practitioners can grasp negative psychic energy within or around themselves or others and send it up to the light. The positive results of this process in healing and well-being are immediately apparent. Reiki aura clearing is taught in Advanced Reiki Training.

Healing Attunement

A special healing attunement has also been developed. The healing attunement uses the same high-frequency energies used in the initiations, but only for healing. This process opens a spiritual door through which powerful, higher-frequency Reiki energies are able to flow and through which the Reiki guides can work more effectively. Because the healing attunements do not initiate a person into Reiki, they can be given to anyone and are especially useful prior to a regular Reiki treatment. The healing attunement process is taught in the Reiki III/Master class.

Three-Step Treatment

A three-step treatment is recommended for those who have taken ART/III Master training. The healing attunement is given first, followed by aura clearing and then a regular Reiki treatment using all the hand positions. This is a powerful combination that speeds up the healing process so that fewer treatments are needed and deeper healing takes place.

Becoming a Reiki Master/Teacher

The Center actively encourages and supports students to become Reiki Masters and teachers if they feel guided to do so. After taking Reiki I & II and taking time to practice and gain experience, individuals can go on to take ART/III Master training. They can then begin teaching on their own as independent Reiki Masters or choose to become licensed by the Center to teach Reiki.

Many take the Master training who do not intend to teach but rather to use the increased healing energies, symbols and skills for their own healing, to help friends and family and to improve their healing practice.

Karuna Reiki®

Karuna Reiki® training is an advanced training course offered only to Reiki Masters. It strengthens their healing energy, allowing it to work more deeply and produce beneficial results more quickly. Eight healing symbols and four Master symbols are taught in two levels. Each symbol has a distinctive purpose and vibration. These additional healing tools help one to be a more effective healer. Karuna Reiki® is the next step beyond the Reiki Master level.

The Center Licensed Teachers Program

The Center Licensed Teachers Program is an advanced curriculum of study that takes at least one year to complete. Students must take all our classes; Reiki I & II, Advanced Reiki Training, Reiki III/Master, and Karuna Reiki® Master, review each class, take a written examination, write a paper and document a minimum of 100 complete Reiki treatments. Then they co-teach each class before teaching it on their own.

To maintain their license, teachers must review classes once a year and turn in class reviews from each student taught. They agree to support the Center Philosophy and Purpose, the Original Reiki Ideals, and to work on their own personal healing. They also agree to abide by a code of ethics and to teach the required subjects for each class. As long as those subjects are covered in class, teachers are free to add meditations or other healing techniques they have found to be useful.

These high standards allow our Licensed Teachers to provide quality Reiki training that is consistent and verifiable. They have also helped us become qualified to offer Continuing Education Units (CEU's) to nurses, massage therapists and athletic trainers who take our classes. In addition, our high standards provide the basis for our plans to work in hospitals and doctors' offices and otherwise interface with the medical community.

If you are interested in participating in our Center Licensed Teachers Program, please contact us and order one of our Center Licensed Teachers booklets.

The Center Philosophy

- Honesty and clarity in one's thinking.
- Willingness to recognize prejudice in oneself and replace it with truth and love. Compassion for those who have decided not to do this.
- Speaking the truth without judgment or blame.
- Respecting others' right to form their own values and beliefs.
- Placing greater value on learning from experience and inner guidance than on the teachings of an outside authority.
- Basing the value of a theory or technique on the verifiable results it helps one achieve.
- Being open to results rather than attached to them.
- Taking personal responsibility for one's situation in life.
- Assuming that one has the resources to solve any problem encountered, or the ability to develop them.
- Using negative and positive experiences to heal and to grow.
- Trusting completely in the Higher Power regardless of the name one chooses to call it.
- Complete expression of Love as the highest goal.

The Center Purpose

- To establish and maintain standards for teaching Reiki.
- To train and license Reiki teachers.
- To create instructional manuals for use in Reiki classes.
- To encourage the establishment of Reiki support groups where people can give and receive Reiki treatments.
- To help people develop and use their Reiki skills.
- To encourage students to become successful Reiki teachers if they are guided to do so.
- To research new information about Reiki and to develop new techniques to improve its use.
- To openly acknowledge the value provided by all Reiki people regardless of their lineage or affiliation.
- To promote friendly cooperation among all Reiki practitioners and teachers toward the goal of healing ourselves and planet earth through the use of Reiki.

Additional Books and Literature on Healing

Reiki, The Healing Touch - *Revised and Expanded*

by William Lee Rand

About the Book

This book was recently updated to include the latest discoveries about the history of Reiki including research from William's trip to Japan. The revised history is based on verifiable facts and includes information from Dr. Usui's memorial stone in Tokyo as well as information from Mt. Kurama where Reiki was rediscovered. The myths about Reiki are dispelled and a clear understanding about the practice of Reiki is established. This book is a must for anyone wanting the latest information on Reiki. It is fully illustrated with more than 40 drawings and 18 photos. It also contains a comprehensive, easily understood explanation of Reiki, how it works and how to practice it. Written with inspiration, clarity and vitality, it captures the essence of Reiki and provides a remarkable depth of understanding. The chapters on *Developing your Reiki Practice, Becoming a Reiki Master* and *Reiki in Hospitals* inspire and instruct one on how to integrate Reiki into the everyday world. It is an excellent introduction to the subject as well as a user-friendly manual for the experienced practitioner. Extensively revised and expanded, this book is over 50% larger than the previous version. It is available in two sizes; a workshop manual for use in Reiki classes and a bookshelf version. Both versions have exactly the same information.

About the Author

William Lee Rand is founder of The International Center for Reiki Training in Southfield, Michigan. He has written over forty articles on Reiki and recorded seven audio tapes. He is publisher of the *Reiki News* and a 130-page Reiki web site. He has practiced Reiki since 1981, and taught full time since 1989. He has received training from seven Reiki Masters and teaches classes worldwide.

Revised Edition

This revised and expanded edition features sections on:

- Reiki Past and Present
- How Does Reiki Heal
- How To Use Reiki
- Detailed information on the Reiki Symbols
- Becoming a Reiki Master
- Developing Your Reiki Practice
- Reiki in Hospitals
- Discovering the Roots of Reiki
- Reiki Training and Licensing
- Photo's of the Usui Memorial and Mt. Kurama
- Extensive footnotes and an index

"Reiki, the Healing Touch is the best book ever written about Reiki. Mr. Rand manages in a few words to capture the magic of Reiki . . . This guideline is a must for anyone who wants to work with the Reiki energy . . . it is THE only Reiki book I can support 100 percent. It is an easy book to read, is well written and makes Reiki available and easy to learn. Thanks to William Rand for this lovely book."

Kari Christine Saether, Teaching Reiki Master

Class Workbook Style — CP401TM $14.95

The Class Workbook is based on William's original teaching manual and is a great compliment to any Reiki I/II class. It is also revised and expanded and contains exactly the same information as the 6" x 9" book. Students and teachers will really enjoy this easy to use 8½" x 11" spiral bound manual that lays flat, when open.

This workbook is used by over 1,000 Reiki Masters as their class manual!

Teacher Discount

Reiki Teachers — order five or more copies of either version and receive a 30% discount on each manual – that is only $10.47 each.

Available in Bookshelf Style — CP401 $14.95

This book is also available in the bookshelf 6" x 9" reading format and has 220 pages. This version is a perfect addition to your library as well as a compact reference book for practicing Reiki. Both versions contain exactly the same information.

Spiritual Healing - Does it Work? Research Says Yes!

by Daniel J. Benor, M.D., Foreword by Larry Dossey, M.D.

This book breaks new ground in presenting research evidence for spiritual healing. Over 175 scientific studies in the area of spiritual healing are reviewed and summarized. More than half demonstrate positive results! The studies involve bacteria, plants, animals, and humans and firmly establishes the scientific reality of spiritual healing. The double blind studies, some of which have been replicated indicate that the positive results provided by spiritual healing involve more than just suggestion and point to a new energy that science has not previously acknowledged. This book presents studies on a wide spectrum of spiritual healing techniques including Reiki and raises many questions about how healing might work in therapeutic settings. This landmark reference book is a must for anyone interested in the field of complementary medicine!

The scientific proof for non--ordinary forms of healing is one of the best-kept secrets of our time. Dr. Daniel Benor has taken the wraps off this immense data base. As physicians and laypersons learn of this evidence, healing may never again be the same. The ultimate value in this information extends beyond healing, however, to touch on the Great Questions: who we are, what our essential nature is, and how we may fit into the cosmos. A majestic contribution in the best traditions of science!

Larry Dossey, M.D.

An outstanding collection of information on healing written by a physician and scientist. Self healing, spirituality, psyche and other modalities are explored. This excellent collection is sure to open minds and help us see all healing is scientific.

Bernie Siegel, M.D.

Dr. Benor's manuscript goes well beyond anything that I have seen in documenting the abundance of work in the psychic-healing field. I am personally delighted to have had an opportunity to review the manuscript prior to its publication. Work such as this needs wide dissemination.

C. Norman Shealy, M.D. Ph.D.

Spiritual Healing Works is a comprehensive overview of scientific investigations on spiritual healing. In this volume, Dr. Benor has assembled data from all over the world. His explanatory theories provide a solid base for badly needed research on these controversial phenomena. The material is clearly presented, masterfully organized and discussed in a manner that is fascinating without being sensationalized.

Stanley Krippner, Ph.D.

Spiritual Healing Works is truly a remarkable effort. This book makes available the literature not only on psi healing but also on other diagnostic and therapeutic modalities. By adopting an energy paradigm, Dr. Benor Brings a coherence to what would otherwise be a confusing picture.

Bernard Grad, Ph.D.

Reiki News

The *Reiki News*, a quarterly publication, contains many interesting articles on Reiki that include information on improving your Reiki treatments, using Reiki in conjunction with other healing techniques and developing your Reiki practice. There are also stories written by practitioners and teachers about their personal experiences with Reiki. A list of Center Licensed Teachers and classes world wide is included. The *Reiki News* promotes the idea of global healing through personal transformation, and honors the value created by all Reiki practitioners regardless of their lineage or affiliation.

The *Reiki News* is also a catalog of Reiki products including: Reiki T-shirts & sweat pants, Reiki books and tapes, new age music, Reiki tables, herbs, candles, crystals, Tachyon Healing Tools, and more!

Index

A

acute illness 84
affirmations 34, 39
Akimoto, Shizuko 119
Alandydy, Patricia 81
allergies 85
angels 31, 32, 38
animals 19
anxiety 69, 82
asthma 84
attunement 9, 16, 21, 23, 24, 25, 33, 34, 44, 48, 148, 149, 150, 170
attunement, additional 33
attunement, for world peace grid 107
attunement, healing 44, 149
attunement, refresher 44
aura 79, 148, 149, 150

B

babies 19
Barnett, L. and Chambers, M. 85
beaming 148, 149
Beaming Reiki Masters 34
Benor, M.D., Daniel 67, 133
Beth Israel Hospital 76
Bishamon-ten 121, 122
bone marrow transplants 76
Bosnia 144
Buddha 23, 31, 34

C

California Pacific Medical Center 83
cancer 68, 76, 78, 80, 82
Cantwell, M.D, Mike 83
Cayce, Edgar 141
CEU 151
chakras 9, 30, 31, 79, 136
chanting 34, 115, 122
chaos theory 100
chemotherapy 83
Chi Gong 34
child abuse 85
circulation 84
class fees 56
classes, time between 55
Clement of Alexandria 89
CNN 138
Cocco, Greda 82
comfort zone 65
competition 39, 99
consciousness 110
cooperation 144
CPR 85

D

distant Reiki 10, 30, 146
distant Reiki for world peace 101
distant symbol 23, 66

E

Earth changes 141
Eisenberg, M.D, David M. 40, 76
emergency-room situations. 85
energy field 6, 9, 30
Eos, MD, Nancy 84
Ethiopia 141

F

faith 53, 87, 88
Foote Hospital 85
fulfillment 63

G

Glasnost 138
global consciousness 143
global consciousness, healing of 142
global healing 9, 11, 101, 146
gnostics 89
goals 63, 66, 80
Grad, Barnard 70
grandmaster 129
Grass Lake Medical Center 85
Guillion, M.D, David 78

H

Halley's comet 141
happiness 53, 99, 115, 143
harmonic convergence 141
Hayashi, Dr. 29, 116, 117, 126, 127
headache 84
healing 138
healing crisis 144
heart attack 85
heart chakra 136
heart transplants 77
higher power 5, 9, 38, 66, 123
higher power, attunement guided 25
higher power, connecting with the 27, 32
higher self 65, 110
HIV 83
hospitals 45, 72, 76

I

infections 84
inner self 64
intention 24, 36, 38, 114, 127
Ishikura, Iris 131
Israel 139
Iyashi No Te (Healing Hands) 116

J

Jefford, Robert 119
Jehovah's Witnesses 142
Jesus 34, 87
Johrei Fellowship 24
journey into consciousness 56

K

Karuna Reiki® 150, 151
Ki 3
King, Dave 119
Koyama, Kimiko 127
Krishna 34
Kurama-Kokyo Buddhism 121

L

life expectancy, global 139
life, purpose of 48
light symbol 122
lineage 21
love 8, 11, 31, 35, 37, 39, 49, 52, 122, 136, 142, 143, 146, 147, 152
love symbol 122

M

Manhattan Eye, Ear and Throat Hospital 76
Mao-son 122
Marin General Hospital 77
master symbol 23, 24, 26, 30, 33, 49, 122, 150
Memorial Sloane Kettering Hospital 76
Mikao 2
Miller, Dr. Robert 71
minister, becoming a 62
miracles 37, 87
Mochizuki, Toshitaka 116
money 38, 41, 56, 58, 63
Monihei, Tanaka 117
Motz, Julie 77
Mt. Kurama 24, 116, 120
musculoskeletal injury 84

N

nerve blocks 84
Northern Ireland 139
Nostradamus 141
nuclear weapons 145

O

Office of Alternative Medicine 40
Ogawa, Fumio 119
Oishi, Tsutomo 119
Okunoin Mao-den 123
origin 160
Oz, M.D, Mehmet 77

P

pain 33, 43, 76, 77, 80, 81, 82, 84, 85
Palestine 139
peace 8, 11, 31, 37, 47, 48, 52, 53, 65, 99, 103, 105, 114, 134, 139, 143
peace, World Peace Crystal Grid 103
Petter, Frank Arjava 119
Peyton, Bettina 85
Phaigh, Bethel 56
plants 4, 19, 70, 72, 134
Portsmouth Regional Hospital 81
prayer 31, 39, 64, 66–114, 72, 115, 122, 142
presidents of Usui Shiki Reiki Ryoho 127

Q

Quinn, Janet 69

R

radiation 83
Radka, Mary Lee 84
rash 85
reality, creating our own 142
Rei 3
Rei Jyutu Ka 116
Reiki and children 18
Reiki and medicine 15, 85
Reiki and pregnancy 19
Reiki community 131
Reiki community, achieving harmony in 129
Reiki, consciousness 35, 49
Reiki, definition 3
Reiki, degrees of 116
Reiki energy medicine 85
Reiki fire 119
Reiki ideals 115, 116, 123, 151
Reiki in Japan 117
Reiki organization 136
Reiki, qualities of 9, 146
Reiki rooms 85
Reiki symbols 22
Reiki, the essence of 11
Reiki treatments 13
Reiki, what can be treated 14
Reiki, who can learn it 15
religion and Reiki 13
research 67, 133
research papers 73
respiratory problems 85
Riggall, Melissa 119

S

Saihoji temple 123
Saltzman, M.D, Amy 83
Samurai 113
scanning 149
schools, hands on healing in Japan 117
Seacoast Complementary Care, Inc 82
secret gospel 89
secret teachings 88
self-hypnosis 34
sensitive areas, treating 60
separateness 99
serenity 110
side effects 19
Siegel, Arlene 78
Soderlund, RN, Sally 78
Sonten 122
Soviet Union 138

Spindrift group 72
spiritual being 148
spiritual growth 140
spiritual path 95
SQUID 70
stress 84
success 63
surgery 80
symbol, power 122
symbols 28, 150, 160
symbols, how to activate 24
symbols, how to draw 27
symbols, secrecy 25
symbols, source of the 24

T

Tai Chi 34
Takata, Mrs. 23, 29, 56, 111, 116
teacher licensing 151
Tendai Buddhism 121
therapeutic touch 68, 69
Toshihiro, Eguchi 117
trauma 85
trust 146
Tsukida, Takichi 116
Tucson Medical Center 78

U

Universal Life Church 62. *See also* minister
University of Michigan Hospital 84
University of Michigan Medical School 84
Ushida, Mr. 125
Usui, Dr. 1, 28, 29, 57, 115, 116, 119, 130
Usui, Dr. , date of birth 116
Usui Memorial 124
Usui Shiki Reiki Ryoho 120, 124

V

Vega, RN, Marilyn 76

W

way of Reiki 53, 65
web of life 100
Wirth, Daniel 69
world consciousness, a shift in 143
World Health Organization 139
world peace 107
Worrall, Olga 71

Y

Yamamoto, Yuki 120